Susanna Elliott-Newth lives in Sydney, Australia and enjoys the pursuits of writing and teaching. As a specialist teacher of children with reading difficulty, Susanna understands the importance of 'opening the reading door' for her students. She writes her sagas to entertain her friends, as well as immerse her readers into the glorious warmth of reading for fun.

This book is dedicated to my husband, Dr Michael Adrian Haines Newth, who taught me how to write, how to use wit as the essence for humour and how to be the master of my pen for entertainment. He was the master craftsman.

Susanna Elliott-Newth

THE LIGHTER SIDE

AUSTIN MACAULEY PUBLISHERS™

LONDON * CAMBRIDGE * NEW YORK * SHARJAH

Copyright © Susanna Elliott-Newth (2021)

The right of Susanna Elliott-Newth to be identified as author of this work has been asserted by the author in accordance with section 77 and 78 of the Copyright, Designs and Patents Act 1988.

All rights reserved. No part of this publication may be reproduced, stored in a retrieval system, or transmitted in any form or by any means, electronic, mechanical, photocopying, recording, or otherwise, without the prior permission of the publishers.

Any person who commits any unauthorised act in relation to this publication may be liable to criminal prosecution and civil claims for damages.

This is a work of fiction. Names, characters, businesses, places, events, locales, and incidents are either the products of the author's imagination or used in a fictitious manner. Any resemblance to actual persons, living or dead, or actual events is purely coincidental.

A CIP catalogue record for this title is available from the British Library.

ISBN 9781398404373 (Paperback)
ISBN 9781398404380 (ePub e-book)

www.austinmacauley.com

First Published (2021)
Austin Macauley Publishers Ltd
25 Canada Square
Canary Wharf
London
E14 5LQ

My thanks go to my wonderful artists: Joshua Brown, Gary Heap, Cathy Stait-Gardner and Cally Brown.

Table of Contents

Preface	13
Privileged Lives	15
Part 1	17
Saga 1	19
The Removalists	
Part 2	23
The Tides of Change	
Saga 2	30
Cold Justice	
Saga 3	37
The Cowboys	
Chapter 1	38
Chapter 2	40
Chapter 3	42
Saga 4	45
The Birth of the Saga	
Saga 5	48
Saga Snippets	
Saga 6	59
Baggage Saga	
Saga 7	63
The Camping Trip	

Saga 8	69
A Sageful Saga	
Saga 9	75
Fuel Crisis	
Saga 10	81
The MUDS	
Saga 11	94
The 5-Star Experience!	
Saga 12	97
You Get What You Pay for	
Saga 13	105
Let Us Reward You!	
Saga 14	110
The Unwelcome Guest	
Saga 15	117
Those Magic Words	
Saga 16	124
The English Teacher	
Saga 17	129
Fair Cop – or Not!	
Saga 18	134
Expect the Unexpected	
Saga 19	139
The Renta Nanny	
Saga 20	147
The Perfect Day!	
Saga 21	151
Road Rage	
Saga 22	155
A Rude Interruption to Her Working Life	

Saga 23 — 158
The Big Day Out

Saga 24 — 165
The Fine Print

Saga 25 — 171
A Conversation with a 2-Year-Old

Saga 26 — 176
The Hypocrite

Saga 27 — 183
A Picture of Dorian

Saga 28 — 188
Loss of Virtue

Saga 29 — 192
'Come on Down!'

Saga 30 — 194
The Reading Debate or Debacle

Saga 31 — 203
Restaurant for One!

Saga 32 — 210
All Things Spiritual

Preface

Michael Newth
1950 – 2018

In loving memory of the very special times I shared with my husband. At no time were we melancholy but instead enjoyed laughter and music. Michael was an accomplished musician and writer of music, as well as a highly acclaimed translator of the epic medieval French manuscripts from the 10th to 15th centuries.

Thank you for being the wonderful husband that you were. I couldn't have asked more of you.

We all lead amazingly privileged lives, and I was so fortunate to spend this precious time with Michael.

Susanna met her husband, Michael, after emigrating to Australia in 1974. They married and lived in Sydney, NSW, where they both taught at the same high school. Michael taught languages and Susanna taught physical education and health studies.

In 2016, they decided to move south to Wollongong, approximately sixty kilometres from the centre of Sydney. On the day they moved, Michael banged his head, which dislodged a brain tumour, which then became active.

Susanna became Michael's carer until he passed in 2018, during which time she experienced many situations that were frustrating. Instead of complaining about the difficulties she encountered, she began writing amusing sagas.

Returning to work at the end of 2018, Susanna was inundated with requests from her friends and family to continue to write her everyday sagas.

All accounts of incidents in this book are absolutely true. Susanna writes predominantly in third person through the persona of 'Susanna' and her husband retains his real name in any of the stories that involve their life together. Most other persons mentioned or portrayed in any saga have been assigned pseudonyms to protect their privacy. The ones who have retained their real names have requested this.

Please enjoy these stories.

Privileged Lives

We are guests in this world:
Souls creating experiences in human bodies.
We aim to bring consciousness into a material form.
To create a deeper awareness of the purposes of each visit.

By understanding this,
We learn the coveted secrets of our earthly bodies
And the journeys our souls make, as we fulfil our purposes
Within the grandiose Action Plan, carefully scripted for each lifetime.

Death is just a passing,
When our souls release their hold on our physical bodies
And escape into an amazing aura of love and light,
Returning Home each time in the sanctuary of peace to review achievement.

Our lives would hold no good,
If the experience was an exclusive barony.
Understanding that perfection is reached through imperfection
Belies the wisdom that imperfection is the ultimate life-long goal.

So, we are guests in this world,
Fully accountable for every thought, deed and promise.
The more profound our metamorphosis, the deeper we love
And appreciate the ultimate privilege of spending time on Earth.

Part 1

Saga 1
The Removalists

> In January 2016, Michael and Susanna moved from Camden in Sydney's southwest to the northern suburbs of Wollongong. A friend of Susanna's had purchased a large family home in this area and needed tenants for her townhouse. The idea of the sea change was an exciting prospect, as the townhouse was within walking distance of the Illawarra coastline. They had hoped to spend their retirement years together by the seaside.

It's official. The Newths are moving!

Family days at the country house were long gone now. Weekends spent cleaning a five-bedroomed house that only Susanna and her husband lived in, as well as the many laborious hours spent keeping the property free of detritus build-up along the perimeter of their little golf course, set amongst beautiful Japanese flowering blossoms, finally made the couple realise that there were more fun ways to spend their retirement time than doing house chores.

Yes, a move would allow the now 'free of children' couple to indulge, get out more and escape to the wilds of the seas at Woonona.

Well, why Woonona you might well ask?

The husband less keen than his wife, but obedient to the end, ended up agreeing – more to please his wife, but also in fear of being left behind. When Susanna made plans, he knew she intended to keep them. His chagrin, of course, was leaving behind his beautiful gardens.

Moving day arrived.

Susanna, as always, took great care in any arrangements she made. However, she could not have foreseen the situation that arose that day. Being more than slightly annoyed by the lies the 'receptionist' had told her about the quality and experience of the gentlemen she had assigned to do this little job, a facet it did not take a high IQ to enumerate within a split second of sighting said gentlemen, she was left with no choice in the end but to grind her teeth and be as helpful and as accommodating to the men as possible.

Now, Susanna is in no way racial. It does, however, help if tradesmen speak the same language. These two removalists had literally just stepped off a plane from their Middle East country and had received no training in how to do any lifting, let alone heavy lifting, let alone conveying a piano from one place to another. Susanna also knew, without a shred of doubt, that these men were quite likely unauthorised citizens, as they could show her no identification, either of themselves, or of the company they worked for.

Their first challenge had been to locate Susanna's residence. Not being familiar with Sydney's road map, the pair had arrived over two hours late, with the sorry excuse that they had become lost – all relayed to Susanna in sign language.

But! They had arrived! They were on her premises and she had no one else – and, they were willing. The day was slipping away.

And, so, she set them to work.

While Susanna and her lovely husband left the job of moving their valuable furniture, beloved piano and other assorted bags in the less than capable hands of the two smiling gentlemen, they sat outside and consoled themselves with tea (the husband, of course, indulging in his usual morning tea cake as well – something he loved, and looked forward to more than anything his wife ever cooked him)!

Hoping to see some progress after an hour of waiting, supping and sipping, Susanna ventured out to the driveway to see the results of the workers' willing labour.

"What are you doing?" she almost immediately cried out in utter despair. Seeing the two men sitting on the miles of beautifully slated driveway leading down the lengthy kilometres of their country estate, chatting to themselves as they wrapped every single item in plastic, and seemingly without a care in the world, Susanna saw red. It was nearly 2pm and the job had been booked to start at 6am. She was understandably exceedingly more than annoyed now!

"Get up!" she yelled.

"Get these things in the truck!" she yelled again.

Not having a clue what the lady was telling them, but understanding perfectly the intent of her messages, and certainly her sign language and bodily gestures, they leapt up quicker than a flash of lightning.

"I didn't order wrapping!" Susanna castigated the not so smiling men now, "And I am not going to pay for it, or the time you have wasted wrapping!"

Susanna then took charge. It was obvious to her these so-called 'removalists' had never removed, or even moved, anything in their lives before. Within seconds she had them jumping on hot stones, each of them not daring for one second to ease up or show her they were too tired to continue (which they were after fifteen minutes – but let up, she did not allow!)

An hour later all items were safely secured in the truck, except the husband's prized piano. The reason Susanna had selected this company was because they had gloated a professional capacity to move pianos in their advertisement.

"Hello – these men have no idea!" Susanna shook her head in absolute fright. The vision of seeing the piano falling from the truck – well almost – had Susanna mustering all the strength she had to prevent it from smashing on the hard-slated floors. Even to this day, she has no idea where that strength came from, or how she had managed to single-handedly catch an extremely heavy and valuable musical instrument, passed down through the eons by such clever composers as Edward Elgar and Benjamin Britten – both gentlemen indeed would have been squirming in their graves, watching her.

All packed and ready to leave. Susanna retrieved the husband, who had slipped next door to enjoy a quick sandwich from the neighbour, who for some reason had felt sorry for him missing out on his usual lunch! Of course, he had willingly accepted her invitation.

"What are you doing?" Susanna had yelled for the second time that day.

"Get up!" Another command, close on her lips.

Finding the husband sound asleep on the lounge, Susanna had nudged him sharply, yelled again, this time more sharply, and then sharply informed him that she expected to see him in the car within two minutes.

Of course, he was!

Part 2

Arriving in Woonona approximately forty-five minutes later, the eager pair had not expected to see their happy-go-lucky removalists immediately. Being patient people, they had patiently sat outside for a while, browsed the shops at Woonona, enjoyed a coffee (cake for the husband) and sauntered back to the house in readiness for the unpacking stage. One always knows the unpacking stage is the easier and quicker of the two processes – how wrong were they that day!

"Where are they?" Susanna had finally phoned the removalist company to enquire about the status of their 'little' job.

"I don't know!" came back the less than courteous response from the disinterested receptionist.

"Well, can you find out for me?" Susanna had endeavoured to sound more courteous than the response delivered to her by the receptionist.

"I'll phone you when I find them," was all she had said.

Did she phone back?

No, of course, she didn't.

Just as all hope was lost of ever seeing their items again, a truck pulled up at the gates of Susanna's new address. Two less than willing workers then appeared at her front door a few moments later, leaving their truck causing a severe obstruction in the street.

"Where've you been?" Susanna had glared at the pair.

"Lunch," the men had gestured an eating action.

"For three hours!" Susanna had yelled this time.

"Is that your truck, mate?"

A passing neighbour was seen angrily pacing towards Susanna's front door, looking fixedly in the direction of the two sheepish drivers.

"Move it," he had yelled. "Now!" even louder.

And, so, without further fuss or ado, the truck was then parked inside the complex in readiness for the unpacking. Let the unpacking begin!

It wasn't that the men were tired.

It wasn't that it was late in the day.
It wasn't that they had lost patience.
It wasn't that they didn't know what was required.
It was quite simply – they had no skill!
They had never done this type of job before.
Within 15 minutes of starting the unloading:

- Both downstairs external windows were smashed.
- Seven large holes appeared in the walls leading up the stairs.
- A total count of 27 potholes appeared in between the seven large holes in the walls leading up the stairs.

Within 30 minutes of commencing unloading:

- Susanna's brand-new leather lounge was ripped on the underneath lining.
- A large hole was made in the side of one of the lounge sections of her brand-new leather lounge.
- The light switch in the hallway was smashed, with glass fragments falling in every nook and cranny of the downstairs entranceways.

Within an hour of the work started:

- The internal garage door, leading to the entranceway, was dented from trying to move the piano in via this door.
- The internal entranceway door was badly dented from moving the piano into the downstairs study area.
- The piano was dented on the top-right corner from being carelessly moved into the downstairs study area.
- Large amounts of paint work were chipped and scratched in all possible areas of the house.

In short, after 60 minutes of unloading all items into the townhouse, the entire house resembled a war zone. As Susanna surveyed the scene, she couldn't fathom how she could tell her friend, who owned the house, what had happened.

Why is it that companies do not want to take responsibility for their actions, or in this case – destructions?

This was the first time in their married life that Susanna recalled her husband not interfering with her decision to **not** pay for work done by shoddy tradesmen. In the past she had always given in to his requests to 'just pay' to avoid the unpleasant scenes at the completion of a job. On this occasion – she had stood her ground, and he hadn't argued with her.

Susanna then explained to the manager on the phone, whose English was, also, not really, good enough to fully comprehend Susanna's somewhat more articulated explanations of what had eventuated. He did, however, fully understand her, when she said that she was not paying for:

- The plastic wrapping – fee charged $250
- The time taken to wrap said plastic around items not requested to be wrapped $500
- Time wasted at lunch $450

She agreed to pay an hour for packing – as that is what it took in the end. $125

She agreed to pay an hour for unpacking – as that is what it took in the end. $125

She then billed the company for the cost of the windows – $250

And in the end the husband agreed to pay for the windows himself. Yeah, he was always such a good boy – he just wanted to make peace!

And in the end, Strata Management for the complex of townhouses, where Susanna had moved to, paid for the internal damage to the house – no cost to the removalist company – lucky boys!

And in the end, the company, of course, did **not** pay the removalists for their day's work, something the two men blamed Susanna for, but which she was not sympathetic!

And at the end of the day, when all items were in place and the house cleaned to its best capacity, Susanna's lovely husband had quietly informed her that (he had banged his head) something Susanna knew was 'a significant event' and one she knew she couldn't change – it was part of his life plan, but she will always ask herself, "Would it have happened if they had remained in their Camden house?"

Susanna, of course, knows the answer to this question!

> After eating a late dinner that night, Susanna had then strolled down to the local beach, just a short walk from her new house. Sitting quietly on the sands, she had written this poem.

January 2016 Susanna and her lovely husband moved to Woonona, a small seaside suburb of Wollongong. On the day they moved, Michael banged his head, which dislodged a hidden glioblastoma. This rapidly grew to 5cm within a three-week period, initiating two and a half years of surgeries and cancer treatments.

This was a journey Susanna was privileged to share with her husband.

The Tides of Change

Susanna reflects on the changes
Her life has encountered this season.
The move to the seaside had brought turmoil
No one could ever have imagined.

The coast with its beautiful beaches
Brought tranquillity and solace
In times when her life seemed without purpose,
Yet knowing somehow there was reason.

The changing tide forced a change in plan
Bringing with it confusion so bleak;
Watching, waiting, wailing and wiping
Her tears as the tide dissipated.

She sat with the seagulls on cold nights
In times when her soul searched for laughter,
And hoping beyond hope of knowing
These feelings at some time would brighten.

In this world, at this time, we have love –
The master of all that gives hope.
She thinks, as she feels the tide turning
Her soul can once again smile a while.

                         This world in which she spends precious time
                                 Changes from summer to spring again.
                         These tides of change now a welcome breeze
                            In her life, bringing hope, love and peace.

Saga 2
Cold Justice

> Having settled into their new home, Susanna decides to continue working for as long as she can. She becomes aware that at some stage in her husband's failing health, she will have to relinquish her teaching commitments and stay home to care for him. For the time being, though, she knew her husband could manage himself during her work absence.
> Susanna works for a large tutoring company in Sydney. She has been employed as a teacher and writer with this company for over three years and really enjoys the dual role afforded her.
> It wasn't until mid-2016 that Susanna decides to leave the company and seek similar employment elsewhere. One of the issues that was forcing her to make this decision was a legal matter between herself and the proprietor of the company. This saga describes the events pertaining to this legal matter.

Mid-October 2014

Susanna was working full-time at the tutoring company. During the morning sessions she carried out receptionist duties, before she commenced her teaching timetable in the late afternoon. The first that Susanna became aware of any situation occurring was when the two owners of the company approached her for a private discussion.

Susanna was advised that the brother of the owner had been arrested that morning at the local airport in relation to a cold case murder that had happened many years previously. He had appeared in court and been granted bail prior to his pending court case. Susanna was being informed of the details of this arrest in case reporters should approach the learning centre at any time.

Susanna had been shocked by this sudden news, that also became local and national news that night.

She was shocked again the next day, when she arrived for work, to find teams of reporters hammering at the entrance doors, eager to speak with the owners. Susanna had simply advised them that the centre was closed, and that they should return when the owners were present. She had then quickly entered and telephoned the owners to advise them of the situation.

Susanna was given strict instructions not to allow any reporters to enter the building and she was to leave immediately and attend an urgent meeting with them.

Feeling somewhat curious, and certainly dubious, Susanna had then made her way to the meeting venue. With so many reporters and camera crew lurking outside the learning centre, though, escaping the throngs of reporters and camera crew had not been easy!

Once she was in the basement carpark, she had been acutely aware of the need to exit the building surreptitiously! She had literally flown down the fire-escape stairs, leapt into her car, and left via the alleyway gate before the reporters had, had time to discover this back – door exit.

Adrenalin pumping, and a slight sweat creeping over her shaking body, she swerved quickly into the main highway and headed to join her bosses. "What had happened?" she had asked herself nervously. She had felt a juxtaposition moment – rare seconds when one experiences complete opposite emotions. On the one hand she had felt exhilarated by the sudden onslaught of unusualness, but on the other – deep concern for her employers, because whatever had happened, must be serious.

And so it came to be that on a cool, autumnal morning in 2014, Susanna sat sipping hot coffee opposite two people she had come to know well, listening to an amazing story that indeed was 'extremely cool' – so cool, it sent icy, spine-tingling shivers down her spine. She listened enthralled to the privy information she was being given, absorbing the enormity of the repercussions that would eventuate as a result of the sudden, unexpected police raid on her employers' family home that morning at 5am. Police raid on the home – all computer equipment and mobile phones seized at 6am. 1st news report issued about the police action occurring in one of Sydney's southern suburbs.

Twenty-five years ago, Susanna's employer was investigated for the death of his brother-in-law but was never charged. 18 months later he was again questioned by police, this time in relation to his first wife's brutal stabbing murder. She had been stabbed by an intruder, who had entered via their bedroom window one night. Although questioned by the police at this time, Susanna's employer had not been arrested and charged in connection to this murder.

The police case went cold after the main suspect in the brother-in-law's murder died. He had been a drug addict and convicted murderer on two previous occasions. The brother-in-law had been suspected of having had associations with various drug syndicates and other underworld organisations. The police alleged that Susanna's employer had paid his first wife's intruder an amount of money to commit the crime, because he owed money to his brother-in-law. This, however, was never proved.

As the first murder investigation went cold, so did the second one. It was only when a solicitor came forward many years later, stating that he was in possession of a letter written by the murdered wife, prior to her death, that the case was re-opened. The letter had read, 'Should my death be unnatural, the police should look at my husband.'

Susanna listened to the story and gave her support to her two shell-shocked friends. She had left the coffee shop and immersed herself in her teaching day.

Over the next week, Susanna's employers had updated her on the events that were unfolding. The employer's brother was released on bail after their mother had paid the required bond. At this time Susanna saw no reason to disbelieve her employer's account of what had happened on the night of his first wife's murder, until…

She is not going to recount this part of the saga just yet…

Other information Susanna gleaned indicated things were not as her employer had explained. When people tell lies, they often forget what these are – the truth remains as fact! Susanna learned:

On the night of the second murder, a man was seen leaving a restaurant that night around nine o'clock. He had supposedly returned secretly to Susanna's employer's house, where the wife was hosting a dinner party. He had allegedly sneaked upstairs and opened the balcony window leading to her bedroom. Then he had checked on the two small children sleeping in the room next door and returned to the restaurant. Two hours later, when the wife at the time had retired to bed, a paid assassin had entered the house via the balcony windows, presumably left open for this purpose.

On this occasion, the assassin was believed to have been paid a large amount of money to execute the deed. After committing his crime, he had fled the scene quickly around eleven thirty, being sighted by witnesses, who had reported, "The man had a knife and was covered in blood."

From November to late December 2014, Susanna's employer continued to chat casually to her about the case. The one aspect of these conversations that intrigued her was the repeated comment, "The police have nothing on me!"

At no time did he ever say, "I am innocent – I didn't do it!"

Susanna remembers thinking this odd. If it had been her, who had been accused, she felt she would have said that…

But…the heart-stopping moment came a short while later. Susanna had been alone in the centre and had just popped out for coffee across the road. Sitting, sipping her brew she had seen her employer enter the building. Quickly finishing her coffee, she had returned to work. As she entered the front doors, she had smelt the aroma of soup cooking – this man always made soup at lunch time and would enjoy his cuppa in the designated lunch area at the rear of the building.

He had not heard Susanna enter her teaching room adjacent to this meal area! He had not been aware either, that she had overheard the phone conversation that he had engaged in with his brother! How does she know it was his brother? Because he had called him by his name!

She had sat bolt upright – ears primed to the wall – not daring to move or even breathe, in case he had heard her. (Susanna is not disclosing the statement she heard that afternoon – clearly evincing his guilt, except to say that knowing it, and then asked to repeat it in court, placed Susanna and her husband's lives in danger at a later point in time!)

With this admission of guilt resonating throughout Susanna's head, she was always on the alert each time this man provided her with updates – she found herself noticing certain body reactions that cemented her belief that he was a very practised and convincing liar. It also concerned her that, on the night of his first wife's murder, he had allowed his two small children to sleep in the room next door, knowing that the arranged event would take place that night.

Susanna had wondered what kind of man this was!

It was March 2015 when Susanna's employer was finally arrested by the detectives, who had opened the cold case. He was detained at a local Sydney jail for six months awaiting trial. When he was transferred to another facility – one that housed long-term criminals, Susanna intervened on behalf of his current wife, as this facility was not appropriate and placed the man in danger. Susanna's appeal to the judge was successful, and her ex-employer was released on bail.

Now in April 2018, Susanna reflects on the continued saga that evolved from the time of her employer's (she will now refer to this man as Adam) release to the court case that commenced in February of that year.

Adam had never shown any gratitude towards Susanna, rather he had set himself up as the managing director of his company and commenced secret negotiations to franchise his company – including a package of ninety-six workbooks written by Susanna. This was blatant stealing on his part, actions that forced Susanna to meet with his franchise lawyers.

This threat of legal action also culminated in Susanna's disengagement from the company, and the decision to meet with the detectives and crown solicitor in respect to Adam's involvement in his wife's murder.

The court case was initially scheduled for May 2017.

A day after Susanna had spoken with the public prosecutor's office, she arrived home to find an intruder had entered her house, checked out the entire lower section, and had ventured upstairs. Nothing had been taken, but Susanna had been aware that someone had entered her husband's bedroom where he had been sleeping. Susanna had thought nothing of it at the time, thinking it may have been her son, until it happened again a few days later. (Her son had reassured her that he had not been around at that time, as he had been at work on both occasions.) This incident occurred on a Thursday afternoon.

The following week, a second incident occurred – this time on the Monday. Adam was aware that Susanna did not work on Monday afternoons. A man, fitting the description of Adam, was seen entering the complex of townhouses, where Susanna lived. The witness could not say how long he had spent in the complex, nor if he was the man who had entered her house that day, but it was obvious that someone had, and Susanna suspected Adam was involved.

The time had been 3.30pm and she had decided to catch the bank before closing time. The intruder entered at exactly 4pm – Susanna's husband had awoken and looked at his clock. Susanna had returned exactly thirty minutes later to find the same footprints all over the downstairs section of the house. Susanna uses floor polish, when cleaning the downstairs tiles, and on both occasions, clear footprints could be tracked going into the downstairs bedrooms and up the stairs.

The prints were clearly that of a man's medium-sized shoe, and a shoe that was a business type as opposed to that of a sport's shoe. Adam always wore business shoes with his suit.

A police report was made this time, and a promise by Susanna to her husband to lock all doors in future. Susanna has absolutely no doubt what would have happened, had she been home that day! The man had not come visiting for a chat!

"If Adam had really known nothing about his first wife's murder, as he had claimed, then how come he actually knew so much about it?" a rhetorical question that had plagued Susanna's mind for three years.

And so, it was with some relief that Susanna listened to the outcome of the six-week trial that finally had closure that day. She had played her part and now felt justice had been served at last.

She had saved her employer from the atrocious conditions of the penal system in 2015, but nothing was going to save him now! So be it. Susanna can now sleep peacefully at night!

That night Susanna wrote this poem, as she reflected on the emotions, she knew he had been experiencing during his initial time in prison, and the fear that had engulfed him at that time, wondering if he would survive the appalling conditions he had been subjected to.

On the Edge

He's on the dark side of an unknown land.
A land where no one cares about his name.
He's cold and lonely – afraid of himself.
He's through with caring…he's through with fears.

The sun comes up now giving way to dawn.
Dawn's cold, crisp air seeping into his bones.
The sun's warmth spying on his huddled form.
He's through with crying…he's through with tears.

He can't remember if he were e'er free,

Free of life's burdens that surrounded him.
Was there ever purpose – did someone care?
He's through with people…he's through with lies.

Is there a dark side on the other side?
Will the bright light await and brighten him?
He longs for something but knows not what.
He's through with waiting…he's through with life.

Saga 3
The Cowboys

Once Susanna had filed a police report on the two break-in incidents, coupled with the uncertainty of not knowing when Adam's matter would finally go to court, Susanna decided it was unsafe for her husband and herself to remain in their house at that time. She was working for another tutoring company and was absent from the house for lengthy times on the days she worked. It was decided the pair would seek other, short-term accommodation.

Susanna found an expansive unit in the south of Wollongong. It was close to the sea and the perfect getaway to accommodate Michael's changing mobility needs. Being fully wheel-chair accessible, Susanna could take him for coffee and walks along the harbour foreshores. They could begin to have some fun together.

> However, once moving in, like many rental places, there were 'jobs' that needed to be done – jobs that had been neglected by the owners – jobs that were the result of damage by the previous tenants and jobs that the estate agents had been lax in attending to.
> I wrote this in preference to complaining about the absurd situation that arose when trying to get some of these 'jobs' fixed in this Shellharbour apartment.

Chapter 1

Tap, tap…

"Hello."

Susanna's ears pricked up at the soft, dulcet tones of a male voice somewhere in the vicinity of her apartment. It is early, too early for any tradies to be on site, and so Susanna dismisses the enquiry.

Stepping outside into the semi-darkness of her courtyard to say hello to her plants, she is somewhat stunned to see a tall gentleman leaning over the railings, peering into her lounge room and drinking from her hose.

"I've come to do yer door luv," he smiles broadly at Susanna.

"Oh, OK," Susanna mildly amusedly responds. "How did you get in?" Susanna asks the pertinent question, an obvious rhetoric given the security gates surrounding the entire complex.

Not a complex question apparently for the gentleman to answer, as he smiles widely at her and announces, "I moved the 'No Entry' sign and came in through the work barriers – too easy!" he beams.

"Well, as you're here, you might as well do the job," Susanna directs him to her front door to show him what needed to be done, instantly regretting her decision when he immediately traipsed outside into the courtyard to look at the exterior light, spreading a trail of sand and cement across the beautiful new, grey carpet and her luxurious lounge rugs.

"Are you going to fix the light too?" Susanna looks hopeful, as he flicks the switch a few dozen times to see if it's not working, which it obviously wasn't at the first flick.

"Yeah, the door and yer front light?"

"What about the back light?" Susanna looks in the direction of her back door.

"What about the back light?" he almost snarls at his customer, but quickly changes his disposition, as business is business!

"It doesn't work either," Susanna satisfies his curiosity, but again regrets the request as she watches the cowboy fill her entire lounge, dining and kitchen areas with silt and sludge. *Great,* she thinks!

"So, what about the door?" another obvious question springs to Susanna's mind, as he inspects the back light in the same cavalier way, he did the front one.

"Oh, yeah – can't do that… needs me mate, as it's too heavy fer me," he stands tall, upright, erect, almost challenging Susanna's even more startled expression. "I'll do the lights, though. Got any globes?"

"Not screw in ones, no. You didn't bring any with you, knowing you were going to fix an exterior light?" Susanna quietly smiles back at the amiable gentleman, who she then recollects has shown her no identification, no evidence of any company name and no job order to verify his presence at her home. (She makes a mental note to be more vigilant in future.)

"I'll 'ave to buy some then," the cowboy now openly looks aggrieved.

And with one last, and very lasting, leer, he strides off once more into the dirt and detritus of the building site on route to his next, no doubt – equally satisfying and successful trade pursuit that wiles away the busy hours on his equally busy schedule of his working day. (Well his boss said he had one, when she spoke to her later that night!)

Chapter 2

Yes, indeed, the boss lady telephoned Susanna that night to advise that her two workers would be unable to attend to her little job until the following Tuesday – a week away, as they had heavy schedules with far more important clients than mere Susanna. She was very polite and apologised for the lateness of the hour.

Susanna bid her a good evening and accepted her decision.

So, it was with great surprise that cowboy number 1 fronted in her courtyard the following morning. On speaking with this gentleman, Susanna reached the quick assumption that this gentleman did exactly as he pleased, irrespective of his boss's organisation of jobs for his benefit!

So be it, Susanna thought, *If he's here, he may as well do the job!*

"I'll get me mate, then," the cowboy smiles.

Dressed in her business clothes, and late for work, Susanna leaves him in the capable hands of her husband to complete the job.

On returning from work at her usual late hour (she works afternoons/early evenings), she could not help but be anything but unimpressed with the sight that greeted her. How did she know what jobs the man, or presumably men, had engaged in during her absence?

Both lights were working – good. A trail of dust and debris littered the walkways to both exterior sections of the house, also leading to the bathroom toilet – but not sink.

"Someone's been sitting on my throne," Susanna papa bear announced to herself.

Someone hasn't cleaned up! Susanna mama bear thought to herself.

And someone didn't wash their hands afterwards! Susanna baby bear grimaced to herself.

Why is it that tradies always feel the urge to expel their waste whilst on someone else's property – couldn't they wait until they returned home? Rhetorical questions that Susanna was fully aware of all possible answers.

Turning her attention to the door work, Susanna could see that the door was on its hinges, had been planned and was operating successfully. The evidence of such activity would be cleaned by her without fuss. (She was just grateful not to have to physically exert herself further when attempting to enter or exit her apartment.)

The phone rang that night at 9pm. (Thursday). Jenny (the cowboys' boss) once again apologised for the lateness of the hour, but this time requested her workers attend the previously planned Tuesday's appointment to finish the job. Susanna, of course, agreed, and as before had bid her a good night.

Chapter 3

It was, therefore, not a surprise, again, to see the smiling cowboy once more attend for work on Susanna's doorstep bright and early the next morning, this time to paint the planed door.

"Does this man even talk to his boss?" Susanna mused, as she greeted him and left for work – today she had business to attend to at her other house and would not be home until late.

On arrival home that night, the cowboy presented himself to show her the paint chip sample that he had been given – it didn't match the original colour of the door, but he used it anyway!

"I dunno what they're gunna do about it," the shoulder-shrugging cowboy said, as he left the building, leaving Susanna with a two-toned painted door.

Epilogue

"How cute – the cowboy has issued an invoice to the estate agent for his services – seriously, is he joking?" Susanna shakes her head in amazement, but quietly thinks – *He just doesn't 'get' it!*

> These cowboys need to fix the door – not expect some mythical creature to magically swoop down into the building and solve a problem – 'they' created!

And so, it was that on the following Tuesday, as originally planned, the two cowboys presented sheepishly at Susanna's apartment to re-paint the door and to attend to any other matters she cared to name.

She kept them busy all day!

The Funfair of Life

> The time that Michael and I lived in Shellharbour Village, we enjoyed ourselves. Michael's condition was steadily becoming more difficult for him, and he was only able to get out and about with my assistance.
> Despite these difficulties, at no time were we morbid or unhappy. For me these were precious times. I treasured every moment we spent together and would not hesitate to experience it all over again.
> One very good service we received in this area was the assistance of the local health service in the Illawarra. The nurses came every day to assist me with the medications, and other specialist staff provided me with training in how to use the heavy lifting equipment. I was becoming 'quite the nurse'!
> I wrote this poem for these nurses.
> Cancer is a beast. There is no other word to describe it. It is callous and uncaring. It grabs a hold and doesn't let go until its victims have no choice except to – let go.
> The poem is a metaphor for this beast. All the rides play their part.

The Funfair of Life

An eerie silence enshrouds,
Closing tightly around
My ears and neck until
I shiver violently.

Big Dipper takes us up slowly,
Inviting us to view
Each changing scene and hue,
Then discards us callously.

I'm asked this question often.
Would I step on again
Knowing the grief and pain
Each ride forced me to endure?

The park is deserted now.
Mirror trees stretch down low,
As a sprinkling of stars
Sparkle in the evening glow.

The funfair, that promised fun,
Inspired an appetite
For magic and mystique,
But only disappointed.

Our lives are a roundabout,
That entices each sense
With each new twist and turn,
Until we're spent and ashen.

The proud carousel horses,
Gracious in their beauty,
Cantering, galloping
Ride us the ride of our lives.

Would you ride again, you ask?
Was any of it fun?
Did you learn, with each turn,
Or were the lessons too hard?

The evil ghost train screeches,
Spectres that laugh and scream;
Vile spit-spats so mocking
Tear tears down faces so cream.

Ferris wheel you wield and deal,
Calculating our risks,
Yet knowing we're safe –
As each high and low we feel.

Lastly, the rollercoaster,
The master of all tricks
Takes you on a journey
That spins so quick, like the switch.

Be careful, though, this monster
Is ruthless and cruel
And cares not for feelings –
It's power that drives this beast.

On reflection of your day,
The cellophane surface
Of the millpond shimmers
In a silky, milky way.

Saga 4
The Birth of the Saga

> As well as writing poems for the nurses, who visited each day, I also shared with them as many funny stories as I could write. These stories were about comical or interesting incidents that happened to me, and they all zealously read them, pestering me for more. Their insatiable appetites for trivia is what gave rise to 'The Birth of the Saga'.
>
> This first one occurred just after we had moved back to Woonona. It wasn't our choice to do so – the building had been closed for renovations, and so we had no other option.

Blown Away

It was a wind to end all winds.

The evening had started cold, with strong, blustery winds howling along the Illawarra coastline, as one of Susanna's lovely nurses battled to keep her feet on the ground whilst walking up the steep driveway to Susanna's townhouse one Sunday night.

Susanna had felt guilty watching the poor lady struggling to manage the steep slope.

> This particular nurse was 'a little overweight' – something she had frequently smiled at Susanna and said, "I don't starve," when Susanna had shown concern that the poor lady was working late and had not had dinner.

On arrival at Susanna's door, the nurse had laughed, "The one good thing about being overweight is that I can't get blown away!"

The pair had both burst out laughing, as the sight of this lady getting blown sky-high would be such a funny and absurd visage.

This lady has a such a great sense of humour, Susanna had thought – the reason she wrote her this saga about her own 'windy' predicament a few days later.

True Story (Wednesday Night Wild Winds)

Today Susanna was literally 'blown away' not only by the fiercely gusting winds that had whipped up suddenly, but by the kindness and quick-thinking actions of the lovely gentleman who had picked up her papers, that too had been caught up in the gusts.

As it was raining, Susanna had erected her umbrella – a particularly large NSW Teachers Federation one, that spanned at least a metre across. Carrying her box of tricks in one hand and the umbrella in the other, she had made her way gingerly down the street.

Just as she was within a snail's pace of the main door of the tutoring centre where she worked, an enormous, gusting beast scooped up poor Susanna, sky-rocketing her several metres upwards Mary Poppins style! Her box of tricks, including all her lesson plans and equipment, went flying around like pieces of debris caught up in a tornado.

Susanna had had no time to react. All she could do was go with the flow.

Fortunately, another teacher, following just a few paces behind her, had seen her predicament and immediately retrieved her lesson materials and box. When these were all safely secured, he had then rushed to Susanna's aid, leaping up to catch her feet just before another violent outburst was about to catapult her even higher into the windy skies.

Landing safely back on terra firma, and in the caring arms of the lovely gentleman who had come to her rescue, two things crossed her mind simultaneously:

1. That he had saved her box of tricks before he had saved her!

2. She was glad she had worn her work trousers and not her skirt to work that day!

But then she had thought, *This lovely man is such a gentleman, if I had worn my skirt, he would not have looked!*

(Every story I write is true and every embarrassing incident is fodder for another story!)

Such is this next saga. Before I include this, though, I'd like to share the poem I wrote for lovely Nurse Linda.

For Linda

When words are not enough,
My thanks seem so insipid.
Enjoy our special treat
With those you love and cherish.

    Remember us with love;
    The conversations we shared,
    The gifts we showered you
    For doing what you relish.

Mike's journey was special,
And I was so privileged
To share this time with him,
As 'twas his greatest wish.

    Love your job with passion,
    And know that all your patients
    Patiently watch and wait;
    By God's grace they flourish!

Saga 5
Saga Snippets

Life is full of interesting, embarrassing and amusing incidents. At least Susanna thinks so. She is never embarrassed by anything anymore – every incident is fodder for a story. Her students tell her she has an amazing life. This concept amuses Susanna as she thinks about the many hours, she spends writing her stories from the solitary, and anything but interesting, confines of her study!

Yes, her exploits to the Great Barrier Reef, where she enjoys scuba diving; the wild and wonderful wilderness of Daintree Rainforest where she flies down the zip lines like Tarzan; the indoor dome in Fayetteville where she is known as 'The Flying Granny' as she deftly soars to great heights – in excess of fifty metres – as she sky dives to the delight of the crowd; or her many and varied experiences coping with Nature's weather, must all seem so exciting to these young children who are just discovering some of these wonders for themselves.

During her husband's illness, though, these pursuits had been put on hold. Instead, she now reflects on the embarrassing encounters she can remember.

The first one she recalls is:

A Matter of Principal

> Prior to her husband getting sick, she had been the principal of a primary school in the Northern Suburbs of Wollongong. This saga is the story of how she came to be appointed to this school and the first embarrassing situation she encountered.

Yes, Susanna is fortunate.

She certainly thought so when she was suddenly advised by the Director of Education to manage two schools.

"Sue, I need a boss at Mary Brooks."

"Oh, are you transferring me?"

"No. What makes you think that?"

"Because you're telling me to go to Mary Brooks."

The man was a man of few words. He had simply said, "You'll be the only principal in the state to manage two schools at the same time."

"So, I get two salaries?"

"No."

He had then walked away.

Fine, Susanna had thought. *I already work a twelve-hour day managing one school. Yes, I can't believe how **fortunate** I am!*

A phone call six months later from the same Director.

"Sue, you're off to the coast!"

"Which coast?"

"The coast of New South Wales."

Becoming a little excited, thinking she might be heading northbound, eagerly enquired further, but all the man said was, "You start in Wollongong on Monday."

"Are you giving me three schools now?"

"No, what makes you think that?"

"Because you're sending me to Wollongong!"

"I'm rewarding you. Be grateful."

"Fine."

And so it was that Susanna left the two schools, one of which she had spent the previous five years, and journeyed southwards to the northern suburbs of Wollongong. Susanna had been well-received in her two special school postings. She had been a specialist consultant in Disability Programs for over fifteen years prior to these principalship appointments and as such had considerable credibility within these two communities of schools. She was well-known, well-liked and well-respected.

This was not the case when she fronted at her new school in Wollongong the following week.

Within seconds of meeting the students and staff, one gentleman had boldly approached her in the privacy of her office with these comforting words:

"I've got rid of four principals before you, and I'll get rid of you!"

"Fine," Susanna had smiled at the man, and as he had turned to leave, had caught his eye and grinned wickedly, "Good luck!"

Of course, he hadn't!

The students found her interesting – a little different from the usual run-of-the-mill principals they had known during their time there. They were so fascinated by her that a contingent of senior students met at the local radio station one morning to discuss the lady with the Morning Show host.

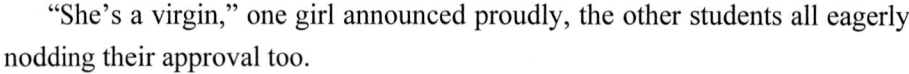

"Boys and girls, do you like your new principal?"

"Yes, the group had eagerly nodded."

"Why? What is different about her?"

"She's a virgin," one girl announced proudly, the other students all eagerly nodding their approval too.

The Morning Show host, not expecting this response, looked at the faces of the innocent children and then around the studio at the cast and crew, who had immediately erupted into fits of giggling, trying hard to stifle the sounds from their radio microphones, before carefully constructing his next question.

He was a little concerned about the volume of calls the radio station might receive that morning – the phones had already started ringing – so he very quietly asked, "How do you know this?"

"Because she told us," one of the boys volunteered.

And with that the entire cast and crew burst uncontrollably into hysterics, immediately turning off any sound that could be relayed through the airways.

"And how did she exactly do that?" the host looked directly at the boy who had volunteered this information.

The children, all six of them, remained quite calm and totally unaffected by the responses of the adults in the radio station cubicle, all looked at the boy as he replied, "She told us she doesn't eat meat."

"Oh, you mean she's a vegan!"

"Yes," the children all nodded, with one girl adding, "She only eats vegetables."

"Well, I'm glad we got that sorted," the Morning Show host had breathed a sigh of relief and instantly switched to music.

Interestingly, Susanna did receive many phone calls that day from several of the local male gentry – businessmen, tradies and others alike – presumably all just 'checking her out'!

As she was driving home that night, three things made her cackle:

1. The radio host had actually believed the students! He just couldn't work out how they knew!

2. That anyone could believe she fronted at the school at the age of 60 and still be a virgin – which they clearly did think! How ridiculous!

3. And if she were – there would have to be a very good reason why, and if that were the case, why did all those 'males' phone the radio station and the school afterwards upon hearing this – did they seriously think they had the 'gumption' to conquer the unconquerable! Obviously, they did!

Again, Susanna muses – how absurd!

A Coffee Catastrophe

The next snippet she recalls is the disastrous two days in a row when she spilt her coffee, embarrassing herself and several customers. The only person who had found the scenes amusing had been the shop assistant who had enjoyed this unexpected entertainment in her otherwise mundane day, not just on one occasion – but two. She couldn't believe her luck!

Susanna was in the habit of purchasing her coffee each morning from the local petrol station. She didn't usually purchase petrol, but on this occasion, she did take advantage of the opportunity to fill up her car.

It was early morning, but the petrol bowsers were already busy, and limited additional car parking space was available for people wishing to purchase shop items. It wasn't really that Susanna meant to be deliberately rude or obstructive – quite simply that there wasn't anywhere else to park!

It was just as she was returning the nozzle to its compartment, that another car pulled up behind hers, instantly demanding she move her car, so that the driver could use her bowser. Susanna had been annoyed by the man's arrogance and manner, and had ignored him, casually turning away and strolling into the shop.

Yes, she had decided to make him wait. She is not usually so belligerent, and certainly would have been obliging, had he not been so extremely rude to her.

Besides, she had thought, *All the parking spaces adjacent to the shop have been taken – where does he expect me to park?*

On making her coffee she had then put it into the microwave, so that it would be very, very hot. As she took it out of the oven, it had tipped over, spilling everywhere. The shop was awash with coffee. She cleaned it up, much to the increasing annoyance of the waiting man outside.

Of course, he had given her, not just the look, but the hand gestures as well, when she had finally returned to her car. Unperturbed, though, Susanna had calmly looked at the man, entered her car and cruised off to work.

Driving into the same petrol station the next day, she was not expecting the same thing to happen.

Susanna could not believe it!

The petrol station was much less busy than the previous day, and there were ample available parking spaces for all customers. Susanna parked alongside the shop, as she didn't need to purchase petrol.

As she began to take her coffee out of the microwave, it again caught the lip of the metal roof of the oven and splattered everywhere. "What's going on?" she had asked herself.

Her coffee had literally ejected sky high – hot, brown liquid soaring upwards and outwards before landing splat, all over a gentleman's crisp white shirt and pin-striped trousers. The cup had then ricocheted onto another man's shoulders, falling eventually onto the floor, also dripping hot, brown liquid down his pristine suit.

To any bystanders watching, the scene was comical, like something out of a weird cartoon clip – not something you'd see in a suburban petrol station shop.

Amused, more than embarrassed, Susanna could only apologise. What else could she do? The damage was done.

Neither man had been amused, though, and so she set about cleaning them both up. Fortunately, coffee without milk does not stain and can be removed with warm, soapy water quite easily, which is what she did. Both men were quite happy to let her attend to them – in fact they seemed to enjoy Susanna's attention.

When she had finished, they had both smiled at her and wished her a good day, both making similar comments about hoping not to see her the next day, in case she made the same mistake a third time.

Having cleaned up the men, Susanna set about cleaning up the shop – she washed all the shelves, a large section of the floor, many of the items stacked on the shelves, the microwave, and the inside and outside of the coffee machine. (Fortunately, there was no irate customer waiting for her to return to her car that day!)

When she went to pay for her coffee, the shop assistant had laughed and said to her, "At least you've left the shop cleaner than when you arrived. It saves me doing it! Thank you."

On leaving the shop, Susanna had smiled to herself and thought, *At least I've made one person happy today!*

The Canny Koala

> To be 'canny' means to be 'shrewd, or smart'. This koala was certainly a very canny koala! This third snippet happened at a time when Sydney had received no water in months. This little koala must have been looking for water because his usual eucalypts were too dry to eat, and he had become thirsty.

Susanna was shopping one day at the local mall. When she heard a rustling sound coming from one of the garbage cans, she was curious and went to investigate. To her surprise, as she peered inside amidst the detritus of paper and food scraps was the cutest little koala – having a picnic. He was only a baby and must have strayed away from the koala sanctuary a few miles from this mall. Once he'd slipped into the bin, he'd been unable to get out.

So much for koalas having discerning appetites, Susanna had thought as she picked him up and wrapped him in a towel. (She always conveniently carries towels in her car boot.) She had then phoned the sanctuary.

As she watched him leave with the warden, she grinned, "This little cutie definitely thinks that left-over hamburgers and chips taste better than gum leaves!"

She just hoped he wouldn't venture back for more!

The Bikies

> Susanna learnt judo and self-defence skills. For a period of time she attended classes run by the police training crew in Hendon, London, UK. Being athletic and physically fairly, fit, Susanna found these skills easy to learn, and she enjoyed the challenges of all combat situations.
>
> From the age of thirteen onwards, Susanna found herself called upon to test her skills in real life situations. For some reason, she knew the 'chosen' one was always 'her'!
>
> This next snippet is a saga about one of these situations.

There have been many times in Susanna's life when she has been accosted by strangers with various intents. She has never been frightened by their invasions of her private space, or their physical presence about her person, but rather, she has actually enjoyed these moments!

"Anyone stupid enough to consider her a likely candidate for any type of physical or 'other' assault is in for a rude surprise," Susanna had smiled to herself one day, after successfully leaving her latest victim squirming in the gutter.

On the next occasion, Susanna had been ambling along a busy main street, lined with holiday makers eating fish and chips and chatting pleasantly in the late afternoon sun. The street led up to a park, which hugged the mountainside leading down to the beach.

Susanna had been chatting to a friend, as the two of them had sauntered casually towards the park.

Just as the pair entered the main strip, Susanna heard the faint sounds of motor bikes. Within seconds, the sounds became much louder and a trio of bikes could be seen cruising into the main thoroughfare.

Susanna, of course, instantly and instinctively knew that this was a staged production – and as well, that **she** was to be the main actor! (How did she know this? She just did!) So, when it happened, she was not surprised.

The three motorbikes carried 6 members of a bikie gang. Parking their vehicles adjacent to the park and blocking all entrances and exits to and from the park, the leather-clad gentlemen adjusted their spurs and portentously stood astride in a horseshoe formation, waiting expectantly.

As Susanna approached the vicinity of their space, she was suddenly pounced on by one of the members, who grabbed her tightly and thrust her into the centre of the horseshoe.

Now, in all of Susanna's instruction and practice, she is aware that strength can play a part in overcoming an assailant. However, not having equal strength to that of a man, Susanna knows she must rely on her skills and techniques to win. She was taught by very tall police officers and so was very used to her practice assailants being fairly, large lads. It isn't size that matters! No, no, no! It's technique, plus the element of surprise – no male ever expects a female to outsmart them – no, no, no!

But she did and has done every time someone has foolishly attempted to try their luck with her.

Susanna is very skilled. Her greatest asset is her ability to remain calm and in control – she really despises people who scream when they are accosted. That gives the power to the assailant. Susanna is too smart for that! She knows to quietly let the scene play out and wait for that opportune moment.

On this occasion, she knew only too well what this play was about, and she was not about to follow the script!

Making her immediate assessment of the situation, she became aware that the entire right-side of her body was immobilised, but that her left arm was loose enough to escape the man's clutches and make an impact on his right clavicle nerve, at exactly the moment he had expected to sink his teeth into Susanna's face.

Even to this day, Susanna laughs when she remembers how her hand had felt, as it had sliced down on the man's shoulders – it had shot up, as if it were made of rubber. The result was that the man instantly passed out, his face passing Susanna's a second later. At first, she had felt silly, thinking that her actions had caused no impact, but when she realised the man was out cold, she had impulsively punched him in the face. She had enjoyed that! She had even smiled to herself at the wonderful feeling she had felt when her knuckles had kneaded his soft, baby-skin face. "He hasn't started shaving yet!" she had scoffed out loud.

That was the moment of terror, though. Up to this point in the assault, Susanna hadn't thought about the consequences, she had just instinctively reacted. From her crouched position, as she straightened herself up, her eyes met the stagnant gaze of the tallest, and most spur-cladded member of the gang. She presumed him to be the leader. Her first thoughts were, *He's going to come after me!*

However, Susanna didn't give him the chance, as she turned away from him immediately – brushing her hands in a suggestive way that said, "She was washing her hands of the situation!" She then resumed her stroll with her friend. Neither of them mentioned the incident as the two headed down to the beach, where they spent twenty minutes enjoying the last of the day's sunshine.

Returning along the parkway, it was just getting dark. In the distance, walking towards them, Susanna could just make out the tall, black outline of the man she had surmised was the bikie gang leader. He'd ditched his bike, and presumably, his fellow bikie cronies for the night and was off in search of other pursuits for his amusement.

Susanna's gaze never left this man's face as he drew nearer. However, to her surprise, when he was within two metres of her, he stepped off the path and turned his body side-on to hers. With a massive swing of his right arm and a long, low bow, he waved her through in full gallant style. It was this gesture that had suddenly turned her legs to jelly.

The man had then returned to the pathway and Susanna and her friend had gone in search of dinner, albeit Susanna still a little shaky!

Joining the throng of holiday makers once more, the pair had decided on chips with vinegar. Her friend had also wanted fish – Susanna not a fish and chip person, had agreed to share the chips.

In looking back on this situation, the only thing that really annoyed Susanna was the lack of action taken by the on-lookers. The streets had been lined with thousands of people – all standing watching. There was a police station next to the park. No one came to her aid! The worst moment of all was when she and her friend stepped into a shop to buy their dinner – the people had glowered at her disapprovingly, as if she had, 'asked' for it!

Staring angrily into one man's disapproving face, Susanna had snorted her silent retort, "Well, thank you so much!"

She and her friend had then sauntered back home, leaving the streets to the holiday makers and the bikies – wherever they were. (She knew they weren't going to trouble her again that night!)

Yes, Susanna certainly leads a very exciting life!

Pictured here honing her skills.
(She is practising with a Walther PPK – James Bond's ladies' gun!)

This incident is only one of many that Susanna has encountered in her life. On reflection, this bikie saga was potentially the most dangerous, as the horseshoe of five other bikies could have come after her. She would not have been able to defend herself against this gang gaggle.

Another potentially dangerous situation was when a middle-aged man approached her one night as she was walking home. As she had rounded the corner leading to her street, he had caught her off-guard, trapping her against a brick wall.

The manoeuvre, she used that night, was exactly as she had practised it the night before at her self-defence class. In fact, Susanna had smiled to herself as he had stretched out his arms in a caged-like manner, thinking he had her cornered. How wrong was he?

Removing the smirk from her face, she had placed her hands behind the man's head, smashed his nose against her upwardly moving right knee, causing him to lose balance, then pulling his right arm downwards, as she followed through with a trip fall, to finally break his clavicle bone.

The defence tactic had taken less than three seconds to complete, leaving the man sore and sorry. He was even sorrier when he was sent to prison. Susanna at no time felt sorry for him.

Saga 6
Baggage Saga

> As Susanna reflects on this saga, it had occurred as a result of a friend of hers becoming really annoyed with her airline of choice, which shall be called Sky-Air, that had created 'baggage' difficulties for her. She had asked Susanna to write a saga about the subject – airline baggage systems. Susanna has no idea what the specifics of her friend's baggage difficulties were, but she came up with this saga as a result of her own enquiries into the services offered by this airline.

Why choose Sky-Air?

Does your preferred airline give you baggage, or does it come with baggage? (This is a pun for those who don't know what 'baggage' is. Baggage is the hassle companies give you when you want to use their services, but the services are not so friendly to use!)

Susanna recently encountered this amusing analogy when attempting to book a short flight with Sky-Air, a little-known, if not actually quite unknown airline to her, that offers cheap flights to many places across the globe. She knows they do offer to fly people to destinations across the globe, as she cleverly discovered their extensive list of world-wide destinations, when trawling through the Sky-Air on-line site recently. However, she also discovered that, to begin the processing point of ordering an airline ticket, required a skill far beyond her simple technological brain.

Her first attempt in selecting the destination, brought her face to face with a smiling face that kindly asked her to select her departure location. (She thought she had done this – apparently not!) So, she tried again. No luck, it seems the computer program only wants her to fly from London, Stansted. Well, she has no objection to flying from this familiar location, after all, she is a Londoner, but to fly there first is going to cost her at least $1500 with another airline.

So, the good lady patiently tried something else. Being reasonably practised at booking airline tickets using computer programs, Susanna skilfully located a booking site that allowed her to fly from a destination of her choice this time. She chose Sydney, as this is her closest airport, and one that surely must afford her the cheapest airfare, particularly as Sky-Air boasts cheap flights. *Her usual airline will always fly her to London for around $550, so let's see what Mr Sky-Air can offer,* she thinks.

"What is wrong with this program?" the patient but becoming not so patient traveller is now thinking, as she attempts many times – more times than she cares to admit in admitting her failure, to type in the name of the destination she wishes to fly to. On her first attempt the smiling face had turned to a frown, informing her that she had not selected an airport.

Ignoring the frown, she then tried again. On this attempt she used the click an airport button to embed this destination into the dialogue box. (Readers, are you impressed with how savvy Susanna is with computer terminology?)

"So, why doesn't this work?" Susanna perplexedly asks herself. "Am I supposed to look up all the airports in Ireland if I want to travel to Ireland. I've never been there, and don't know which one will be the closest to my hotel. Is this why this airline boasts such cheap flights – their passengers must do all the leg work?" Surely not, even Scoot give their passengers a list of available airports to choose from, even though there is no way in a million years Susanna is ever going to 'Scoot' across the globe. (She's having serious doubts now about this Sky-Air option!)

"Let's try one more time," the ardent, seasoned traveller smiles to herself. Well, she might as well smile, as Mr Sky-Air's crew was now only giving her stern warnings about continuing to use and subsequently abuse the computer systems on their site.

"Hmm! Let's try phoning this company," Susanna finally decides on this course of action after successfully receiving three brown frowns, but unsuccessfully selecting a place to fly to, resulting in a warning not to continue to use the site if she isn't a serious traveller.

"Yes, Good Morning, I'm trying to book a flight to Ireland. Can you help me?"

"No, we have an on-line site for you to make your bookings."

"Yes, I tried that."

"So, what was the problem?"

"I didn't know what airport I needed to fly to."

"Punch in Dublin, and a whole suite of options for Irish destinations will appear. You can then choose the option of your choice."

"Thank you for your help. I'll certainly try that. Just out of interest, though, do you charge for baggage, and how much can I take?"

"Yes, we charge $100 per bag up to 15 kgs. Oh, no sorry – we've recently given **you** a bonus by decreasing our fees to $80 and increasing **your** luggage capacity to 20 kgs. You can take as many bags as you like, but it is cheaper to pay for baggage when you book – will that be all?"

Susanna was actually impressed by this man's ability to make it sound as if this airline was doing her a favour by giving her gifts, particularly as she has never needed these **gifts** with any other airline she has ever used before! Signing off from the pleasant-speaking gentleman on the phone, Susanna reflects on her morning's work.

To book with her usual airline using her airline points = $770 with 23 kg of baggage took 3 and a half minutes.

To book with Sky-Air will cost her (no idea – she was never able to reach the payment page) plus $160 baggage return, with a lengthy phone call to the airline – total 3 and a half hours.

It's probably just as well she's not flying to Ireland in the near future!

This Life

As Susanna is busily putting her sagas together, her husband clearly shows signs of regressing more quickly. It was at this point in his health needs that she decided to give up her work and become his full-time caregiver.

Before she continues with her own stories, she would like to share one of his poems. Michael was a translator of Old French Medieval manuscripts from the era 10th Century to 15th Century. He was the only translator world-wide who preferred the verse versions to prose. Being a language lord, he loved the assonance and alliteration his artform created, and he was praised highly by leading professors across the globe for his skill in retaining the original meanings of the texts when translated into English.

This Life

This life is not my native land.
This mortgaged lot of heart and hand
With lease of mind to understand
This life is not my native land.

This world is not my native place.
This mortgaged plot of time and space
With peace of mind to know in grace
This world is not my native place.

My living world is far away.
Beyond the gates of night and day,
Beyond the straits of come what may
Where now I bide but will not stay!

Michael Newth, 2016

Saga 7
The Camping Trip

> Susanna, now settling down to her new routine and spending more time at home, she enjoys reflecting on times spent with family and friends. This next saga was when a somewhat 'dizzy' friend of hers invited her to go camping with herself and her four children. Susanna calls this lady, 'Dizzy Miss Lizzy'– aptly named because of her 'happy-go-lucky-ways'!

I wrote this story for Mel (Melissa) and Kylie who work at my fitness centre, after they invited me to go camping with them. I was always amazed and amused at why these two young girls, only a few years older than my daughter, would insist I went 'clubbing' with them.

"Don't you have mums of your own to ask?" I would laugh at them.

"Sue, you're not like our mums," they would laugh back.

"I'm more like a gran," I would again smile wryly at them.

No, I never went clubbing – but I did go camping! Kylie arrived after I had left that weekend, so I didn't get to spend time with her and her two boys. Mel's kids were enough!

Setting Off

Susanna has been camping before. Those days of camping rough on cold, windy Welsh mountains were etched still vividly in her memory.

She had liked those times, getting up at 2am to beat the competitive army traffic. Her little group of Outward Bounders was exceptional – five girls all eagerly eating up the dangerous mountain routes, as if they were on a Sunday stroll along the well-worn Blue Mountains bush tracks – and with packs weighing 40 pounds!

Yes, Susanna's group was tough, because she as their leader expected them to be tough. At the end of this extremely arduous program to build resilience and leadership skills, Susanna was selected as the number one candidate by an outdoor pursuits program to be part of a trek to the Himalayas the following year. Not only was Susanna the first selected candidate of only twenty participants to be selected in any one year, she was also the youngest ever to be selected.

So, Susanna has skills. She is not averse to camping!

When her lovely friend, Dizzy Miss Lizzy, invited her to join her family on an Easter weekend camping trip, Susanna was happy to accept. The weather was glorious and so promised to be a lovely escape to the peace and quiet of Pretty Beach, south of Nowra, NSW.

And so, it was agreed that Susanna would meet the lovely family at a designated intersection on their route south, and, like in her Outward – Bound days, she prepared herself early and set off.

Waiting for over half an hour was no real problem for the lady – she happily amused herself listening to her songs, but once the hour struck, Susanna began to have second thoughts about the merits of this trip.

Just as she was about to return home, the Corby van arrived.

"Hey there! Sorry we're late!" a smiling face beamed at Susanna as Mel's car parked alongside hers.

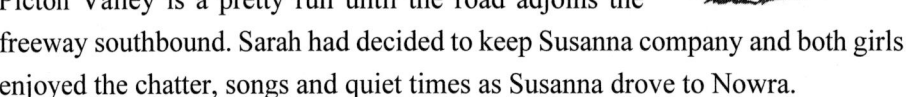

Yes, they were finally off! Heading through the Picton Valley is a pretty run until the road adjoins the freeway southbound. Sarah had decided to keep Susanna company and both girls enjoyed the chatter, songs and quiet times as Susanna drove to Nowra.

Now, Susanna was not expecting much direction – and indeed she would have been surprised if too much pre-organisation had occurred, but she felt some notion of when they were going to stop and have a break was of modicum importance, as after two hours of driving plus the hour wait in her car at the start, prompted her need for coffee!

"Let's stop at the Nowra Maccas Mel!" Susanna had telephoned her jovial host.

"Yep, great idea Sue. See ya there!"

"Are these kids really gunna eat all this?" Susanna looks gobsmacked at the mountains of food being placed on their table and asks herself if this was just morning tea or lunch. She sips her coffee while she watches the hoardes devour their feast.

"Yes, they were – and they did!" Susanna smiles and seriously wonders what kind of a weekend she is in for.

"Let's hit the road, Mel," Susanna directs the crew, "Before it gets dark," Susanna directs her attention to the huddle of children, she felt needed direction, as she hustles them out of the restaurant and into the waiting cars.

"Yep, Sue, but the boys wanna have a turn with you. Here Mitchell, get in the back and Christopher you get in the front."

"Nah, I'll get in the back with Mitchell."

Mitchell at this time was only about 4 years old and his brother, Christopher, a few years older, but younger than their sister Sarah, who was fourteen.

Oh, goody! Susanna thinks. *Perhaps I shouldn't have offered to stop for coffee!*

And, *Oh, goody*, she thinks again immediately she drives out of the carpark. *Not only am I the taxi service now, but I'm host to two noisy, joke-telling, fa_ _ _ _ _ boys who find amusement at the slightest road sign, animal they catch sight of, person walking along a street or tree they see!*

Needless to say it wasn't long before the usually calm and patient Susanna felt the need to stop her car and issue the errant boys with a brief expectation statement, a few carefully chosen words to let them know she was 'becoming' annoyed, and an idea of what might happen to them if their behaviour persisted.

Needless to say the remainder of the trip took place in absolute silence, with the two boys too scared to open their mouths to breathe, let alone speak. "Ah, the joys of being a teacher! I know all the tricks," Susanna smiles as she enters the camping site carpark.

Setting up Camp

"Mum, where are the tent pegs?" an annoyed Andrew scowls at his mum. Andrew, the oldest in this clan of 4 children and the one who clearly sees himself as the 'responsible adult' with his dad not joining his family on this trip.

"Dunno – oh! Yes I do, they're in the garage waiting to be packed!" Miss Dizzy Lizzy smiles at her son. (Now we know why she's earned her nickname!)

"Oops! I'll go and borrow some off friends here!"

While the dizzy one goes off in search of tent pegs, the other three children see an opportunity to escape and check out the social scene, ne'er to be seen again – at least until the tents are up! (Smart move on their part!)

On returning with a handful of pegs, the cranky one, getting crankier by the second, again asks his mother where the mallet is.

"We have one somewhere!"

"Who is going to help me put this tent up?"

"I dunno – where is everyone?"

"Mum, this would not have happened if dad were here!" Andrew had stormed off leaving his mother to put the tents up by herself.

At this point Susanna had seen her opportunity to escape too. She had wisely decided not to actually camp on the beach with 'the family' but had sought a nice, quiet, little cottage in the bush about five kilometres off the main road. As she has already mentioned, she is not averse to camping – however, she does like good organisation, her own space and her own food!

"Ah," she had breathed a smile of absolute pleasure, as she had breathed in the salty-sweet air of Pretty Beach. *Good decision*, she thinks as she drives out of the camping grounds.

The little cottage was perfect, nestled in the trees and fronting onto a lake. Susanna is a writer. She loves writing. It is her greatest pleasure. She never misses an opportunity to write, especially when her surroundings are so conducive to her creative juices.

Setting up her laptop and writing materials facing the lake, a kangaroo hopped up to join her. *Perfect!* she thought as she fetched him some bread.

Susanna was well set up. She had everything she needed for her three-day get away. Making herself a sandwich and allowing herself a deliciously cold glass of her favourite sparkling white, she settled down to write for a few hours.

Feeling the chill in the air, she stretched, made some coffee and then decided to join her hosts for a social evening of wining and wiling away the beautiful sunset hours as they farewelled the sun on Pretty Beach – aptly named.

"The sun will be back tomorrow," the moon smiled as she appeared gracious as always, and so happy.

"But was the family happy?" Susanna had mused as she had noticed the disarray in the campsite. Yes, the tents were up. Yes, assorted eskies were scattered in walkways, bottles of wine were opened and inviting her to drink. "Thanks, I won't say no," she had eagerly poured.

Yes, the family was as happy as they were going to get that weekend. A pleasant evening sat drinking and chatting made memorable memories for Susanna until it was time for her to head back to her little cottage.

Slipping into bed that night, she had felt at peace with the world and her life.

She slept like a log – well she actually slept on a log in front of the fireplace – a fire that she had lit the previous evening that glowed softly over her as she slept peacefully. The ambience in the room was calming, until…

"Ah! Far – out!" Well that's not exactly **what** she yelled at 3am!

Turning on the light she saw the largest huntsmen she had ever seen in her life crawling over her bedding. He too had wanted the warmth of the fire and had crawled out to keep her company.

"Out! You're going outside!" Susanna had yelled at the spider, and fetching a broom, she had flicked him out onto the paving areas of the verandah. She had then blocked all doors with draught excluders to make sure the beast didn't re-enter.

"Ah, now I can get back to sleep," Susanna smiled.

(But was she smiling a short while later?)

Breakfast

"Knock, knock. Sue, are you there?"

"Oh, no!" Susanna stirs in her blankets, cuddled up by the grate like a blanketed walrus. "How did they find me? What time is it?"

Glancing at the clock on the wall, she notices it is just past six am. Outside the sun was also just rising – a little lazy, as was Susanna. *Well it's still a bit cold at this hour, so I don't blame him,* Susanna thinks.

"Knock, knock. Sue, are you there?"

This time she knows the intruders are not going to go away, so she reluctantly forces a smile to welcome five hugely smiling faces peering into the windows of her little cottage lounge room.

"Hey, Sue, we've come for breakfast," was all they said.

"Great, come in. We'll cook pancakes!"

"Great," the happy, smiling clan all say.

Within seconds Susanna has them all working – some finding cutlery, others finding plates, others mixing batter, others frying mixture, others eating fried mixture, others washing up – all as Susanna watches and directs.

Within seconds the room had gone from a quiet, peaceful, early morning sunrise to a noisy, bustling thoroughfare, with even the sun calling in for his share. The day was warming up!

As the group sit munching happily on pancakes with lashings of syrup, eating up every last scrap of fried batter, Susanna looks across at her friend.

"Mel, your children are unusually well behaved!"

"Sue, that's because I told them you'd smack them, if they didn't behave!" Mel grinned back at her friend.

"Why couldn't you smack them?" Susanna had retorted.

"Because they're more scared of **you**!" Mel had just laughed.

"Great!" Susanna had stood up to wash the remaining dishes. "I'm in for treat of a day!"

Epilogue

The day was great. The kids were great! The sea and sun behaved themselves and everyone had the perfect day at the beach. It hadn't been Susanna's choice to return home that night, but her husband had needed her.

Yes, she was glad she'd camped – well, gone camping at least!

Thanks Mel Corby! You have a wonderful family!

Saga 8
A Sageful Saga

> Now that Susanna was home full-time, she did everything she could for her husband, and she has no regrets. There are some things she kept secret for reasons known only to her. This saga is an illustration of a secret that, had she disclosed to anyone, would have brought contentious arguments from both her husband, as well as his family.
>
> Susanna had been given information from a friend about a clinic in Los Angeles, America that specialised in herbal remedies and treatments for cancer patients. Not usually in favour of any such 'quack' treatments, in this case she had been impressed by the successful results this clinic had boasted and decided to make the trek.
>
> As a result of these treatments, the couple had two and a half very special years together – he had only been given 3 weeks initially. Susanna thinks that we do what we **have** to do. She told him she was going to Brisbane, which she did. (She just omitted to tell him she was flying further afield afterwards!)

He knew she was flying to Brisbane. What he didn't know was that she was then flying a few nautical miles further on to Los Angeles. He thought his lovely wife was staying with her close friend, Annette, in Brisbane. Well she never actually said she was staying with her only friend in the world – he just assumed she was – as she  was going to Brisbane for the weekend. He knew she was going to fetch him a treatment program, and for that he was grateful and supportive.

Leaving home at 9pm on the Friday night, Susanna trekked into Sydney to camp at a nearby hostel to catch the 6am flight to Brisbane. The husband, perfectly understanding his wife's predicament of possibly not being able to find a South Coast train at 3am, supported her decision to leave him to his own devices on the Friday night. After all, he had been left some delicious culinary treats to tide him over the weekend – little sweeties that warmed his heart and gladdened his soul.

Yes, his wife could go! "Good-o!" she had thought and left – this ploy had worked.

The flight to Brisbane had been uneventful, as was the long haul to Los Angeles an hour after landing at the domestic terminal. Arriving in LA at 6am, she collected her luggage and proceeded to customs.

"Ma'am, where's your luggage?" The very, official custom's officer glowered at Susanna.

"I don't have any, as I'm not staying the night."

"Don't you like our country?"

"Yes, I like it just fine – I just don't have time to stay the night. I'm travelling back to Sydney tonight."

(At this point Susanna suspected the custom's officer thought she was trafficking drugs but was confused as to why she was so brazenly giving him clues.)

"Yes, I'm here to pick up a consignment of drugs."

"So, don't you need a case to put the drugs in?"

"No, because the company packs the vials into special bags for me," Susanna had smiled.

Needless to say, Susanna was machine-body searched on the spot, taken to a special room where a female attendant full-body searched her and then asked her to display every item she had with her out on a table. (Yes, a full body search involves finger penetration, for those who were wondering, or had never had such an experience at customs before!)

"Ma'am, how can you come into a country with only one small bag? Where have you hidden the rest of your luggage?"

"I'm only here for the day," Susanna explained again. She then outlined to a group of officials, her plans for the day. Of course, they didn't believe her, phoning both her day hotel and the well-being centre to check out her story. When they returned from their checks, Susanna received a simple, "Good luck, ma'am." (There had been no apology for the poke!)

Breathing a huge sigh of relief and exiting the large, international terminal, Susanna's next challenge was to hail a taxi – one that wasn't going to charge her exorbitant rates just because they knew she was a tourist. She only needed to travel about 500 metres to her day hotel. She could see the building from the terminal doors, but there was no walkway access. The taxi route, Susanna observed on the dashboard, read 10 kilometres with a flat rate of $25. Susanna had not been impressed.

However, once in the hotel, sitting in her room, she had thought, *This is Heaven!*

Her hotel was a place to shower, eat, sleep for a few hours and then head off to her appointment at the medical facility north of the city.

"Is the concierge available?" Susanna approached the reception desk a few well-rested hours later.

"Can I help you, ma'am?" the receptionist looked affronted at Susanna.

"No thanks, I was asked to ask for the concierge."

"And who asked you to do that?" she again snorted her retort at Susanna.

"A friend," Susanna smiled back.

As Susanna waited, she couldn't help thinking, *What does it have to do with her who I wish to speak to?*

But, being the absolute perfect traveller and hotel guest, she simply smiled sweetly when the young girl returned and stated, "He'll be with you shortly, ma'am."

Suddenly, just as Susanna was thinking no one was going to meet with her, a very handsome, and extremely tall young man flew down the stairs and raced into Susanna's lap – literally – he tripped over a lobby chair, landing smack in the middle of her chest. Picking himself up, and being extremely embarrassed, he apologised and adjusted his clothing.

Susanna had tried hard not to laugh, even though it must have looked somewhat comical to any on-lookers.

"You must be Susanna," he eventually smiled, regaining his more normal demeanour. "My friend said you were wanting an Uber to take you up Sunset Boulevard."

Susanna was given instructions where to meet the driver and so she set off.

Now, readers, try not to be too jealous of what Susanna experienced next.

Susanna has been to Los Angeles many times, but she has never actually been out of the airport vicinity before. Shaking hands with her driver for the day, she had felt like a celebrity as he had waved her into his waiting luxury sports style car, sparkling in the carpark of a very expensive – much more expensive – hotel than the one that was her home for the day.

"Susanna, I just have to pick up another guest – he's actually a friend of mine, and he wants a lift near where your appointment is – I hope you don't mind."

Settling into the car, Susanna said, "Perhaps I should sit in the back then!"

"Oh, no. It's okay. He won't mind sitting in the back!"

The driver then wound down his hood, switched the engine on and chatted incessantly until his other passenger arrived.

"Just call me 'M _____,'" was all the friend said, as he shook Susanna's hand and jumped into the back seat. (Susanna cannot reveal his name for privacy reasons, she can only hint that it is someone somewhat famous.)

"Show Susanna the sights, Devon."

Devon did. He drove Susanna up Sunset Boulevard, pointing out all the famous beach spots, carnival areas, cafés and restaurants, as well as locations where famous film shots had been recorded. The two men had chatted enthusiastically to their Australian guest as if she were the 'famous one', until Devon dropped off his mate at his rendezvous.

As Devon had driven off, he had looked boastfully at Susanna. "He always has me drive him when he's in town!"

The Well-Being Centre

I bet many famous movie stars and models visit this place, Susanna thought as she entered the lavish, up-market suites of treatment and consultation rooms. This place had been a referral from a friend of hers, who had also visited this place for cancer treatments – highly recommending it.

For the adventurous traveller, the idea of meeting with this doctor with a difference is an exciting concept. Specialist oncologist, turned spiritual healer, turned chiropractor, turned herbal therapist, this unusual doctor has opened a clinic in LA that specifically treats the causes of cancers. Susanna has journeyed this far to see what this man can offer her husband.

Five hours of gymnastic manipulation, including an excruciating chiropractic workout, and an immensely enjoyable head laser zapping treatment, Susanna farewelled the good doctor, armed with a mountain of herbal remedies to catch her flight back to Brisbane.

Arriving back in the Custom's Hall, Susanna wondered if exiting Security would be easier than its entry.

Fortunately, it was. Customs seemed uninterested in Susanna this time, even armed with all her array of pills of every possible type and culture. She graced graciously through all checkpoints, grabbed some coffee and sat down to quietly enjoy the memories of her amazing day.

It was all surreal. Her head was in a spin – and it wasn't the wine!

She felt so special as she boarded her flight home, sipping Champagne and enjoying a well-earned meal – she hadn't eaten all day.

And sleep she did, arriving back in Brisbane in time to catch her scheduled flight to Sydney on Monday morning, when her lovely husband was expecting her back, greeting her warmly,

On being advised about his new treatment plan, he had been sceptical at first, but had soon warmed to the idea of this holistic, herbal remedy, particularly when his lovely and caring wife had gone so far (Brisbane he thinks is a fair way) to get this treatment plan for him. Be grateful, he must now be, and embrace these multitudes of pills with enthusiasm and gratitude.

Four weeks later, the monk (Michael's nickname) is performing well at his book signing event, turning up early for his IV treatment, and smiling widely at his oncologist who tells him his bloods are perfect and his heart is in Olympic condition.

Hey, something must be working. The oncologist had advised the good doctor and his wife, a month earlier, that there were no more chemo treatments available for brain cancer! Life expectancy had been estimated at 3 weeks.

Yes, the trip had been worth it – Susanna's efforts and funds had increased his life and time with her, and the quality of his life had been increased too, as the remedies cleansed his organs and prevented him from getting any infections.

So, well done, Susanna!

I wrote this poem on my trip home from Los Angeles.

A Moment in Time.

A Moment in Time

Our lives are fleeting glances
Within infinity of time;
Like passing stars we flicker
Then fade to other realms.

Through eons of space we sail
With purpose and dedication,
Striving to achieve our goals
In fields of come what may.

We pass this way many times,
Exploring galaxies unknown;
Each glance a different reason
And purpose to fulfil.

Like snakes shedding outworn skin
Our ethereal souls surge onwards
In the ever-flowing ebbs,
That guide our births and deaths.

Mourning loss of loved ones
Brings much sorrow and great sadness;
Be comforted in knowing
We journey Home when done.

Saga 9
Fuel Crisis

> Landing safely back in Sydney, after her clandestine trip to the United States, Susanna is reminded of a time when she visited her daughter, who lives in Savannah, Georgia, U.S. Susanna's one fear in making her journey to the Medical Centre on Sunset Boulevarde, had been the fear of any incident occurring that would cause her plane to crash. No one knew she had made these plans – no one would have known who she was – and her family would have been left devastated at not knowing what had happened to her.
> So, on landing safely, Susanna had been immensely grateful. All was well again, and she now hoped her husband would be too, armed with his array of pills for every possible well-being function.
> In reflecting on the trip to see her daughter, Susanna's husband had certainly known she had made this trip, but had he known about this saga, he would never have allowed his wife to venture on to any plane ever again – for any reason!

The flight to Los Angeles was uneventful, as usual. Susanna is a seasoned traveller, always carefully selecting her seats and her meals on any flight she books on-line. And so, arriving in the big, international airport – the gateway to the U.S. – was not a particularly exciting interlude for her to look forward to – she has been here many, many times in the past ten years.

After Susanna had retired from her full-time position in a school, she purchased a house in Savannah, Georgia. Why this town? Well, it was where her daughter's husband was stationed prior to his deployment to Afghanistan.

Joshua Brown pilots helicopters and is an exceptional pilot, leading his crew of apaches in every training exercise organised to keep the American military officers in peak condition until D. Day.

At the time, Susanna was able to buy a brand-new two-story house for under $180,000 AUD, which she knew was always going to be a good investment. (She had no money afterwards, though, but the relief of not worrying about where her daughter would be living was worth the loss of stress!)

So, Susanna could now come and go anytime she liked between Australia and the U.S.

Since her daughter has moved to America, she has lived in all the states her husband has been transferred to. American military staff are required to move every four years. Susanna first visited her daughter in North Carolina before she and her husband moved to Alabama and then settling in Savannah. Savannah is an historic town – the oldest in America.

It is famous for its old houses and nightly visiting spectres. If you wander down River Street, you can still see the young girl, who waits at the entrance to the merchant shipping lanes for her long, lost sailor boyfriend to return home. Her body has now turned to stone and a single trickle of tear runs down her snowy-white cheeks. It is a sight for sad eyes.

"Thank you, ma'am – you're good to go!" the nice, young passport checking officer smiles at Susanna.

"And, thank you. That's good to know!" Susanna cheekily returns the smile. "Y'all have a nice day now!"

Yes, she must practise the drawl now that she's heading east and then south. Next stop – Atlanta.

Susanna likes Atlanta. She often stays in a hotel there when she wants some privacy. It is only a short hop to Savannah from Atlanta in a little Embraer – a plane she enjoys being a passenger on. These small hoppers are ideal for short travel, and she always selects the best seat at the front of the airplane.

The hour was late though when the LA/Atlanta flight landed. The airport lounges were empty and becoming quite chilled. Without the bustling throng of people and shops open to keep the atmosphere warm and friendly, the air and ambience was becoming uncomfortably cool.

Susanna seated herself in one of the available lounge chairs – her flight was not full, so there were plenty of available seats. It was about 1am when her flight was called to board. By this time her flight group was the only mass of people still left in the entire airport. On hearing the announcement, everyone (except Susanna) charged to the gates, pushing and shoving, grunting and groaning, wheeling and pulling, snorting and sniffing as they made their way through the checkpoint and onto the plane.

As the last passenger before her had successfully passed through the barriers, Susanna gracefully graced her way to the awaiting flight attendant. She had no need to hurry – her seat was right at the front of the plane and, as she had no luggage to lug, she could breeze along and sail swiftly and stylishly into her awaiting special seat, which she did.

"Oh, no – bugger!" Susanna suddenly looks up at the larger than usually large airline captain that had snuck onto the flight after her.

"Where did he come from?" she asked herself. She hadn't seen him waiting in the lounge.

"I dunno where I'm gunna sit," he smiled pitifully at the flight attendant. "I sure as hell won't fit in that, there little seat, they've allocated me!"

The man was immense in stature, and when Susanna turned to see where he had been designated to sit, she completely understood his predicament.

Breathing in a huge sigh and emitting profanities only known and heard by her lips, Susanna quietly stood and said, "Captain, you'd better have my seat."

Susanna is always the perfect passenger.

"Why thank you kindly, ma'am – much appreciated," his grin broadening like a Cheshire cat – for two reasons:

1. He got the best seat in the house and
2. He got to chat up the lovely flight attendant.

And so – the flight took off.

Soaring eloquently into the well past midnight skies, the air was becoming unsettled, as cumulus clouds could be seen building – even in the darkness. There was an ominous feel in the air as the plane pushed the clouds out of the way in its ascent to safer realms.

Susanna, forced to sit in the captain's designated seat, was now right at the rear of the plane, and over a winged section. She could feel every bump, engine thrust and shake – and shake the plane did, gently at first – and then massively so.

"Passengers, this is the captain. I don't like this plane and I'm returning to Atlanta. Sorry folks!"

Turning around and heading home – Atlanta is Delta's base – the plane was hastily flown home to bed. Once more sitting in the cold, deserted airport lounge, the passengers were a little quieter this time. The excitement of the flight had dissipated, and tiredness had set in. People lolled around on the hard, plastic seating or lay sprawled on the floor. Susanna sat patiently in her seat and attempted to message her daughter, who was waiting at Savannah airport to meet her.

Susanna's daughter usually waits at home until she sees the Atlanta flight take off before heading to the airport, only a twenty-minute drive west of her house. On this occasion she had left earlier, expecting her mother to arrive around 11pm. With her oldest child, Xavi in the car, she had thought he would sleep as she waited. However, now at almost 2am both of them were awake and worried where their visitor was.

"Folks, you'll be glad to know a plane has been found."

Yes, Susanna thought. *I am.*

This time boarding wasn't quite such a schmozzle! The tired passengers began queuing as directed in a more orderly and patient fashion – Susanna once again the tailender. Taking off, as before into the skies, the weather had deteriorated considerably in the last hour. Bolts of lightning could be seen in the far distance to the south.

Great, Susanna thought. *That's where we're going!*

Suddenly an enormous bang resounded off the side of the plane near where Susanna was sitting. It was too dark outside for her to see what it was, but – whatever it was, made the plane shake and then fall a few feet.

"Sorry, folks. I'm going back. I don't like this plane either," a tired and unhappy captain once more advised his throng.

Disgruntled passengers erupted immediately into overt discussions, but Susanna knew there was nothing gained from getting cross. This plane had been sitting in a hangar for a reason. She just hoped the next one would be in better shape.

And so once more the group assembled in the waiting lounge of the Delta terminal in Atlanta. No one spoke.

"Folks, I've arranged for a plane to be flown to us from Houston," the captain approached the sprawling mass of people.

"I'll get it fuelled quickly, so we can get you folks to where you need to be."

Again, no one spoke. Few even looked at the poor, frustrated man.

Susanna thought, *He too wants to be home.*

It was around 4am when a plane finally, now full of fuel and passengers, flew off into the skies Savannah bound. Looking out of the window, it was still dark, and stars graced the skies, but it wasn't the stars that mesmerised a tired and very hungry Susanna – she doesn't eat when she's travelling, and she had been travelling now for over thirty-six hours non-stop. It was the flashes of lightning, that were causing her concern. From her little backseat window, Susanna could see a massive thunderstorm immediately over Savannah airport as the little Embraer approached.

"Bugger," (that's not exactly what the captain's expletive was) a downright annoyed captain had suddenly exploded into his microphone.

"Sorry folks, Savannah airport's runway lights have just gone out. This means we can't land – we'll just have to circle until they fix them."

"Well, 'bugger' wasn't the word the passengers used either on hearing this announcement," Susanna smiled as she listened to the assortment of word choices from around the globe. English blasphemes are different from German ones, and different again from U.S. ones. She smiled again as she thought about the different nationalities of people who were on-board. She estimated nine different cultures as tourists and a couple more as now U.S. residents. "Oh well," she grinned to herself. "That exercise passed the time."

The plane circled eight times before the captain spoke again.

"Folks, they don't know what they're gunna do with us, so we'll just keep circling. We have fuel enough for another twenty minutes."

As Susanna sat thinking, she remembered her son-in-law had said that planes carry a spare twenty minutes of fuel after the gauge reads empty.

This is comforting, she thinks. *Has this plane only got that much, or is there still twenty minutes of fuel before the gauge reads empty?*

The plane circled for a further forty minutes. Susanna had been keenly eying the progress of the plane around every circular track, spotting the familiar landmarks of the mountains, seascape and airport. She looked at her watch – it was almost five-thirty.

Her daughter would be beyond being worried. She wondered if anyone had told the waiting cars about their predicament, or even their estimated time of arrival – she supposed not. The storm outside the plane was still sparking and growling furiously. There would be no way any technician would be out there fixing the runway lights in this weather. Just as Susanna was becoming seriously worried about the fuel situation, the captain bellowed out, "They want us to go to Jackson. Hell, I'm not going to Jackson. They can go take a leap!"

So, the captain kept circling. Susanna kept worrying. The plane kept flying. *At what point would it just drop from the skies?* she thought as she sweated profusely in her seat. It was freezing in the plane, but her fearful disposition was making her shiver from fear and not from the cold. She didn't care how freezing it was – she wasn't going to die of cold!

"Folks, we are just about out of fuel and so I'm going back to Atlanta. I can't wait for these idiots to decide what we're to do any longer." A very tired and very cranky captain aired his grievances publicly on his PA system.

Ah, Susanna thought. *We now have twenty minutes of fuel left. Atlanta is forty minutes away. Good luck!*

There are no words to describe how Susanna felt when the plane finally landed at Atlanta Airport at 7am. She watched the fuel trucks pull alongside the plane and desperately hoped her daughter had returned home. She looked at her watch. It read 7.30am and her plane began taxiing out of the gate.

"At last, we're on our way." Susanna smiles a tired but now relieved smile.

"No, we're going back! Why?" Susanna watches the plane retrace its steps to the gate.

"Um – what can I say," the captain suddenly yelled into his microphone. "They've put the fuel in the hold. Do they seriously think I'm going to fuel in mid-air?"

Susanna smiles wryly as she observes the captain doesn't apologise anymore for his use or rather 'over-use' of the 'f' word said now after almost every word he's using. "He's given up being polite."

As Susanna watches the fuel trucks once more draw up alongside her window, she wonders why the captain feels it's necessary to tell his passengers every detail of what is occurring. She decides it's because he is just so annoyed at the whole sequence of events, he just wants to vent his wrath.

Savannah Airport 8.30am. The passengers disembark. Susanna hugs her daughter and Xavi. They had both sat in their car all night.

"Why didn't you go home?" Susanna asks her daughter.

"Because the car has no gas! I wouldn't have had enough fuel to get back here."

Susanna doesn't say what she'd like to say, but instead just smiles at the two of them and says, "C'mon. let's fill up and go home!"

Saga 10
The MUDS

> The M.U.D.S. is an acronym for The Macquarie University Dementia Society group of people, who were my husband's colleagues at university. They affectionately called themselves this, as they began to gracefully age. They were the first French Language intake of the university, and a group of about fifteen members kept in touch with each other throughout their lives.
>
> When Michael became sick, Susanna organised many functions with them to share happy times and memories. Some of these special occasions included coffee excursions, lunches out and weekends away.
>
> During this time, Susanna wrote many poems and stories for this group, some of which she would like to share here as a tribute to her husband.

Ode to the Weather

The wild, windy storms that greeted the residents of the Illawarra on Sunday 5th June 2016 will be remembered for many years to come. Torrential rain cascaded down the buildings like giant waterfalls intent on doing as much damage as they could in a short time. Along the usually peaceful shoreline savage seas swelled high, and with such velocity that the people walking along the promenade were drenched by the surging tide, being caught unawares by the unusualness of this cyclonic storm.

On this day Susanna had a house party. Here is the poem she wrote for her guests at the end of a tumultuous weather day. People came from Canberra, Goulbourn, North Sydney and the Blue Mountains overcoming obstacles insurmountable. Some of them made it – some didn't, but it's a day those that did – will truly remember.

As the sun sets on the Illawarra escarpment
Susanna reflects on the enigmas of the day.

Those poor cold souls who fought the water at Waterfall
Whilst waiting for the city folk who had battled trees,
Debris and an assortment of detritus
To reach the Illawarra coast.

And poor Catherine, like Lawson and Wentworth who trekked out
In inclement weather to find those social pastures,
That only a wet, wild and woolly Sunday
Can offer as any solace.

Then Gail, like the gales that ravaged the Southern Ocean,
Blown from the Outer Hebrides of greater Sydney,
She bravely braced against such terrible storms
To arrive in delightful style.

The day had started wildly, like never seen before.
The sun too ashamed to show his face, hiding from view,
As the gusting, cyclonic winds sought revenge
By wreaking havoc for hours.

Looking across at Black Mountain – this foreboding mass
Of granite so dark, glares angrily at each victim
Who dares to venture forth and challenge his might,
As mighty he is – there's no doubt.

But end, the day does, as it started – blowing fiercely.
Susanna hopes by now her guests are snuggly snoring,
Weary from their wanderings, but contented
In knowing that they made it home.

The next day, when she inspected her property, enormous trees had been uprooted – trees that had been there for fifty years. Yes, it was a day to remember!

Kiama Downs

This poem is a memory of a wonderful weekend spent in beautiful Kiama on the south coast of NSW with the MUDS.

The cove lies waiting.
At this hour nothing stirs,
Not a moth's spray,
Not a gnat's whirl;
Just the dark and quiet.

The sweeping grasses,
All freshly mown
With no snail's slime,
Wave to their visitors.

The Rock – the Granite,
So powerful and strong,
Stands tall – watching –
His wise knowing
Keeps his secrets locked tight.

Such pure perfection
Graces Nature.
Her beauty proud
To welcome the day – trippers.

The day birds slumber,
As mist enshrouds
This hamlet town
Where sea greets sand
Then dissipates again.

Kiama Story

After this successful weekend, Susanna invited her husband's family to share a similar experience. Instead of writing a poem, she wrote them a story that contained their names. These are highlighted in red.

In deep night the cove lies waiting.

Nestled, sheltered between the lush green hills and the Granite, a massive mountainous range so powerful, it sends signals of contrition to all who gaze upon him. At this hour in the morning, the Granite stands majestic amidst the rising mist and early morning dew that seeps into his bones making him shiver slightly.

His guests will be arriving soon. He must look his best.

Below the Granite the waters of the cove and inner harbour flick flecks of sparkling gems, glistening like beautifully fermented white wine, reflecting their images on the surface of the moon. At the water's edge, mirror trees stretch down for the moon and a sprinkle of stars – their midnight parties now giving way to slumber, as dawn approaches.

There is no sound in the cove, not a single **Buff** or puff from the incoming tide, not a fish swirl, no insect scrape or gnat's scratch, and no hint or **Tone** of any changing hues.

But something is happening… very slowly.

The Kiama Harbourside Shack

In the **Hart** of the cove a faint line appears on the water, nothing more than a trailing of a straw. As the moon slides towards the Granite, a small knob pushes from the water, and gleams in the soft light. The moon now dips behind the Granite, leaving the night to the stars.

The knob becomes a point, a beak, followed by the green head of a bird. The bird has heard of the guests who will soon be arriving.

As the early morning light sweeps the last star from the sky, a shining head sits in the water and stares at the silent mountain in the **Derek**tion of the harbourside, a few metres along the **Marg** where the cove's guests will soon gather. (A marg is a street.)

A curious fly drones, also in anticipation of the new arrivals to the cove, and drifts around the green bird now sitting outstretched on the water, drying out in the warm sun. The fly hovers a peck away from its curved beak, but the bird is not interested. He is only interested in the guests.

He sits up facing the Granite, looking through the cleft, cut by a **Cleaver**, along the winding harbourside thoroughfare, across the **Gruber** mine shafts, through the wine plantations, past rickety fences thin with sheep and cattle, over grey-slated roof-tops and along the freeway… to a blink in this anything but barren land…

To a row of small cars growing bigger as they turn into the cove.

The Cove smiles a wry smile… His guests have arrived.

1. Derek and Margaret Hart
2. Liz Cleaver
3. Tony Gruber

The Dreaded Deluge

> It was just after Easter, 2016 when Michael had recovered from the first of his three brain tumour operations. To celebrate, Susanna invited all his family and friends to join them at the Novotel in Wollongong for a smorgasbord lunch.
>
> This occasion was also a fundraiser to raise a donation to the Cancer Council for their wonderful assistance in providing Michael with daily transport services to his radiation appointments.
>
> To add some fun to the events that Susanna organised during these two years, she created the 'persona' of 'Susanna Tours'. Guests would arrive at functions and inform the establishments that they were guests of 'Susanna' – and of course the proprietors would smile politely and say, "Yes, of course you are!"
>
> On this next occasion, however, the weather was so wild and changeable, that it made for an even more momentous occasion. Susanna wrote this poem for her guests the next day.

The dreaded deluge predicted for the Illawarra coastline,
Was a knife and forkful shy of descending upon
The assembled guests at the Northbeach Novotel yesterday.
The first entourage, lured by the delicious aroma of freshly brewed coffee,
Ambled down with ample time to settle in before
The onslaught of assorted offspring arrived in style to dine.

Susanna Tours, as her guests couldn't fail to prevail, and be impressed by,
Is well known in these parts, which once recognising
Acceded them the invitation to indulge the chocolate box goodies with gusto.

Sitting and chatting with his familiar family, Michael
Was anything but a knife and forkful shy of
Culling any of the culinary offerings so deliciously placed before him.

As the empty seats gradually welcomed their guests, sighing a smile –
They were glad to offer a comfortable and relaxing repose
In that social interlude between morning tea and luncheon.

And what a luncheon it was, with plates piled with detritus
Of every scale and scallop, scoop of soup or splash of hash,
As knives chatted and forks talked throughout their gastronomical journey.

At first, feeling forgotten, the pavlova had demurely mused,
And then become bemused, when she was suddenly
Thrust into the limelight, along with the lime and pie ice-cream, to perform.

Spying on the indulging early risers, she had not expected so much attention,
But was proud and delighted to queen their bowls none the less,
And her guests were certainly impressed with every delicious mouthful.

One highlight of the afternoon, worthy of note, or of noting worth,
Must surely be that distinguished garb, that eloquent accoutre
That complemented Michael's stylish attire, attracting so much attention.

One guest in particular, unable to resist the impulse a while longer,
Attacked the cravat, drawn no doubt by its crevette couleur,
Looked equally as eloquent on him as it did on its esteemed owner.

With the weather uncertain as to whether to rain, hail or what,
Decided instead to play safe, and allow the guests to retreat homeward
Before it reminded them that its storms were forecasted to be ferocious.

Susanna and Michael sincerely thanked their guests for joining them,
For sharing this interlude of changing times and tide;
And for their genuine care, love and much-appreciated, never-ending gifts.

Thank you everyone.

Magic Magenta

It was later in the year that Susanna organised the two weekend getaways to the Central Coast of NSW. Michael's family had enjoyed a quiet weekend at Magenta before the large group of MUDS descended upon these shores too.

It was an open-house style five-day weekend, with people staying for two or three nights over the five-day period. The only stipulation Susanna had made was that each person was responsible for one meal. The Susanna Tours brochure had boasted golfing, tennis, casual indoor swimming and croquet on the lawns. However, every guest throughout the entire weekend was much happier boasting around the bar stools at night, strolling along the beautiful beaches during the day, casually sauntering and sipping their wine at the winery tour on the Sunday morning and sitting cross-legged on the lawns at the end of their busy days chatting heartily with a laugh – or two. Whatever they did, they had fun!

The Central Coast, with its pristine beaches
Is an idyllic getaway
To zealously anticipate.

This MUD's reception is a special time
To celebrate a year of strife
And ever-changing treatment plans.

The Magenta Shores Resort is unique,
Boasting pursuits for every age,
Race, creed or muddle-headed MUD.

How often in life do we get the chance
To relax with friends and drink wine –
Then dine in style by ocean views.

Susanna Tours has a few surprises
Up her sleeve for the active ones,
With the main aim of having fun!
So, look forward with eager excitement
To this splendiferous event,
And celebrate with Susanna and Michael.

A Prayer of Hope

> Saying farewell to 2016 was a welcome acknowledgment of the achievements Susanna and Michael had surely realised through their efforts – medical, surgical, therapeutic and social. They were both enormously thankful to all the medics, nursing staff, family and friends who, kept the equilibrium positive and happy at all times.
>
> As the year turned over, Susanna wrote her friends this note and poem.

Since being home Michael has seemed to make daily improvements. Yesterday we saw the medical oncologist who was delighted and relieved to see Mike's progress. He told him he would see him next month. You can't imagine how we both felt. He even decreased the steroids. We are both stoked! To begin the new year with such hope is all that we both hoped for.

Your prayers have touched our hearts
And humbled us beyond reason.
When all hope was lost, we hoped
To see the changing season.

I lay at night with such fear
That our lives would change forever,
And I would wake in mourning
When each new day saw dawning.

It broke my heart to see him
Lose the things that made him happy.
I prayed that when the time came
The end would happen quickly.

Your prayers, my friends, were heard,
And we can't thank you enough.
Our days are filled with beauty
And a love beyond compare.

For Sures

> The next two years brought Susanna and Michael closer than they had ever been before. Living near the sea, they spent every day strolling along the walkways and beach tracks. Early in 2018, when they moved to Shellharbour, Michael began to need more equipment, and certainly a wheelchair. 'For Sures' was written on the foreshores of Shellharbour Quayside after they had settled into their new location.
>
> Despite all Susanna's efforts to provide her husband with the best care, she could see the signs of deterioration and a loss of interest in what this world had to offer him. Susanna's job, though, was to keep him as happy and as comfortable as possible.

The tides of change have turned once more,
Bringing a new landscape to Newth shores.
So bewildered by these changes,
Susanna and Michael smile for sure!
Renovations, adaptations,
Commodes, walkers and chairs – so much more.
Mike's changing needs changing daily
Bewildered Susanna – that's for sure!
A prisoner at home in bed
Was no life for the monk, anymore.
No more, no more Susanna cried,
When all that was left was selfish pride!
He'd thrown out books – music all gone –
Left with nothing to do, he cried poor.
So, the winds whirled, and the seas turned,
Sailing the pair southwards to new shores.
A wheelchair's walk to harbourside,
With cormorants, ospreys, albacores.
The fresh sea breeze not felt in months,
Heartened spirits – he smiled now – once more!

Susanna

La Fin des Temps La Fin du Monde

Michael's favourite words when the rains pelted, and the winds whined were:

La fin des temps la fin du monde – The end of time the end of the world

When rains do fall as heavy they sheet,
He lies awake 'tween sheets for days.

When losing mind as sure he is,
He lies asleep for fear of wake.

His movements now seem old and worn –
His knowing eyes too tired to weep.

La fin des temps – la fin du monde –
What is the point he asks himself?

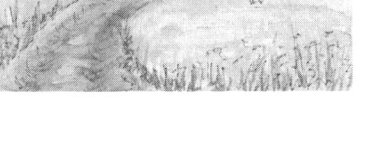

The juxtapose of life and living –
A paradigm or paradox?

His confused state, he must admit,
Confuses him beyond his realm.

With sun comes hope, like fresh mown grass,
That's freshly dewed – he breathes once more.

Susanna

The Gift of Suffering

> Michael left in early August 2018. In 2017 he had finally finished the last of the old epic manuscripts from the medieval era, and Susanna, family and friends had celebrated with a momentous book signing event. He had been so proud to wear his monk's garb, and Susanna has been his lady.
>
> Throughout his life Michael had translated many tomes, never before having been translated from the old French to poetic English as 14-line sonnets. Michael's skill, and the one that set him aside from all other translators of this type of genre, was his musical and language talents.
>
> He was a language lord and fine musician. His translations were poetic, but accurate to a 't'.
>
> It's what he came to do – and having achieved this phenomenal success, he left.

We enter the world upside down
And journey through life backwards.
We cannot know what lies ahead,
As this would destroy all purpose.

We only see where we have been.
The mistakes we've made are clear,
As we survey each passing glance
In our journey on through life.

We suffer pain to understand
How to grow in soul and strength.
So, treasure hardship – welcome strife
And celebrate your journey.

God selects each gift with great care,
To help and guide us with love.
Rejoice when times are troublesome,
And know His gifts were special.

Susanna

Infinity

> This final poem in this section depicts the connection that Susanna has with her husband. They had met as planned, and Michael had departed – as planned.

I am that tiny speck of light that sneaks through the horizon at dawn, sparkling like a jewel before opening the door to day.

I am that crisp bite of morning that strikes so sharp like a whetted knife, piercing so cruelly but awakening you to life.

I am that moment of truthfulness - the dilemma between right and wrong, that nags at your conscience, racking your guilt, until ousted.

I am that flicker of new tide that brings new hope and beauty so rare, glistening like Heaven's milk, embracing your emotions with love.

I am the pin-point of high noon – that peak – that fastigium of power, soaring rays like stingrays, grabbing at senses and burning breath.

I am that second of twilight – that magic moment when lights go off, before stars shine brightly, and night in all his splendour - reigns king.

I am that final second of life, when Nature's sleep allows you to dream, but wake again supreme in Heaven's harmony of light.

Susanna

Saga 11
The 5-Star Experience!

> With Susanna now free to go and visit her daughter in the United States of America, Susanna booked her flights. As there were no trains to the airport at the time she needed to leave, she was forced to stay the night before at the airport hotel on the concourse of the international airport.
> This next section of this book is dedicated to amusing stories that Susanna wrote to entertain her friends. They are written purely for fun and not to be taken too seriously! The 'f' word is themed throughout, as a language device – a symbolism – representing just how ridiculous a situation can be.

Susanna is sitting in the lobby of a large, Sydney hotel adjacent to the international airport wondering what constitutes the award of the highest star rating. There is a reason she is contemplating this beyond the usual boredom of sitting alone with idle thoughts, passing time.

Is it the size of the building?

No, move on from that thought…this building is very large – one might even describe it as more than necessarily large, draping unnecessarily over the airport sidewalks forcing arriving and departing guests to lug their luggage into gutters of every depth and width while they scan its widths for signs of entry.

Where are the f…ing doors to this monstrosity? While the hotel boasts close proximity to the international airport – the building she agrees, certainly is close, but are the doors? After walking around for more time than Susanna would have liked, she eventually did locate these pokey glass constructions, which, she might add, caused her more than the usual red-faced embarrassment, as she poked, prised, tapped, slid, knocked, knocked more loudly and then finally, did nothing – opened ceremoniously slowly when the sweetly, smiling bellboy simpered,

"Madam, they open by themselves."

Susanna had then graciously and gracefully entered.

Is it the efficiency of the check-in staff?

No…this crew is no more or no less efficient and artificially sweetened than any other she has encountered at any of the other, similar lodgings she has previously stayed in.

Is it the smartness and general demeanour of the clientele who stream through those easy – to use – automatic doors that Susanna had struggled with?

A definite 'no' here. Seriously, did all these people choose their attire carefully, or did they simply throw on the first glad-bag cast-offs otherwise destined for the 'op-shops', or did they all dress in the dark?

Looking around at the higgledy-piggledy assortment of people from all walks of life, Susanna smiles as she recalls her own carefully selected items and even worrying whether her wonderfully comfortable sandals would be suitable!

Glancing up at the arrivals board to see if these people had arrived from interesting source locations, Susanna wonders if the ratings arise from airline choices – are these the big-wigs or Scoot!

Scoot! Is this even an airline?

These passengers have come from SN – where's that?

As Susanna glances outside to critically assess further arriving passengers, she is suddenly amused at the sign on the transit bus – 'Free transportation to the international terminal.' Is this for real? Who would be that lazy?

I can see the entrance doors from my current seated position in the hotel, she scoffs loudly, attracting unwanted attention – so quickly, and quietly keeps her thoughts to herself.

Is it the facilities in the hotel?

Gym: no – there's no – one here! There're all in the bar stuffing themselves with all the accoutrements the hotel and their budgets afford!

Laundry: no – if I'm coming home, why would I waste time now washing when I could be sleeping – the most urgent need! If I'm going away, which I am, my beautifully packed, carefully selected, vacuum-packed and pristinely, clean clothes don't need washing!

Room Services: possibly!

Are there any? Susanna wonders as she searches for a cup, spoon, glass, jug – would be good – tea bag/coffee pod! Rummaging through all possible drawers, she locates a single cup and tinier than tiny jug, with an even more tiny chord.

"Where does this plug in?" Now cackling beyond normal sarcastic cackling that she soooo enjoys when she travels, she tries hanging the base and jug upside down from the only available electrical port for the purposes of heating water, but gives this idea away due to the obvious result of water pouring downwards onto the carpet.

"How totally, bloody stupid is this?" (I should have taken a photo!)

Is it the bed?

Yes!

And yes, again, and yes – the upgrade was worth it, and yes, she slept and yes, she smiles as she heads off to check – in and grab a quick coffee. And 'yes' there is one coffee shop open! She was told there wasn't! (She is reminded never to listen to the advice of others again!)

Saga 12
You Get What You Pay for

Once more into the breach dear friends! Susanna has finished her teaching schedules for the term and she's heading north to warmer climates.

Well actually, Susanna has 'no' friends and so technically, she is writing this saga for no one! She thinks, though, that possibly in the future she might acquire one of these 'rare commodities' thus making this exercise feasible.

The subject of this saga is quite simply, 'You get what you pay for – there is no such thing as a free lunch!'

Companies are out to get your money at all costs. Companies creatively devise cute, catchy slogans and tacky taglines to lure us into their trickery. Of course they want us to buy their products – and of course they don't want us to get these products cheaper than their set prices – and they certainly aren't giving them away free – but they do try soooo hard to give us the impression they are doing us a 'favour'!

Arriving at the airport terminal Susanna is suddenly bombarded with a multitude of slogan options for her to take advantage of.

2 4 1 (Two for One)

"I don't want two, so can I please have one and just pay half?"

"No, ma'am," came back the terse reply.

We Have You Covered!

"Covered for what?" Susanna asks the rather young, airline receptionist seated immediately under this large statement.

"Well, actually Mrs Newth, we don't have you covered, because you haven't taken out any travel insurance with us!"

'More Bang for your Buck!'

(Susanna has seen this slogan used by used car salesmen but never on a billboard outside a café)

"I'd like one of your bangs for a $1 thanks."

"We don't sell bangs, ma'am, we only sell coffee."

"Well, then I'd like a coffee for a dollar."

"Coffee is $7.50 for a small cup."

"So, what's the bang?"

"You get a free cup on your coffee card on your 10th cup!"

"Oh, right! So, you get the bang – that's $67.50 I have to spend to get a free one!"

'We sell the sizzle – not just the steak!'

"What does your slogan mean?" Susanna asks the owner of the fast-food outlet.

"It means our steaks are soooo juicy, we leave you with that 'sizzling' feeling."

"Hmm! At 4am I think I'll pass, thanks."

'Think Different'

Yes, thanks Apple. Good advice. Now I'm beginning to see why.

'I'm Lovin' It!'

I'm not! This McD café coffee is luke, warm, much too strong and much too expensive. This small cup of long, black decaf has set me back $6.50. For an extra $1 I could have bought the coffee card at the other place!

Perhaps the coffee on the plane will be better!

As always, Susanna is the epitome of the 'perfect traveller'. She knows exactly what to take and how much, and so she is not encumbered by baggage, and all her needs are at hand. Wearing carefully selected garments that depict the smart, but casual traveller, Susanna boards her flight.

'You're the reason we fly!' (Seriously! They take off into the skies a thousand times a day – just for me?) Hang on – didn't they used to use, 'We still call Australia home?' Where else would they call home? They're an Australian airline!

Susanna ponders about this change in slogan, which probably also means a change in company direction. "Oh, well, as long as this plane is heading in the direction of Queensland, I'll be happy!"

The seasoned traveller enjoys her flight and arriving in Brisbane quickly exits the terminal building. She then treks across to the train station for her journey to Roma Street, where she is told – the parklands are worth strolling through.

"Well that would be fun, if it weren't so f _ _ _ _ _ _ freezing and wet!" (always looking for the alliteration) she shivers as the 14° C temperatures smack her in the face.

"That'll teach you to come up here!" the wild, windy beast continues his onslaught about her countenance, snarling nastily at her.

I told her to take an umbrella!

And I told her to take her jacket!

"Yes, these parklands can wait for another day!"

The hotel is satisfactory. "Does it meet her expectations?" something Booking.com will ask her at the end of her trip.

The room is alright. "Booking.com could you not have organised a noisier, or more-busy, room?"

The purpose of Susanna's getaway is to write – writing requires quiet, peace and time alone.

'Knock-knock!'

"What would you like?"

"Nothing ma'am – I'm here to ask if there's anything you would like."

"I'm good, thanks."

"Yes, but is there anything you need?"

"I'm right, thanks."

(Has this young fella just stepped off a plane from the UK? He has never heard of these expressions before!)

Seeing the confused look on the young attendant's face, Susanna smiled and said, "No, I have everything I need. Thank you."

Susanna always leaves her front door open, likewise her hotel room door. She smiled as the young man sauntered off in search of the next victim for his services. She is reminded of the first time she entered a shop to buy items when she came to Australia. In a strong, striny (Aussie strine/slang) accent, a young girl had glared at her and forcefully exuded, "Yer right?"

"Emma chissit?" Susanna just couldn't help herself. She had been reading 'Let's Talk Strine' on the plane. Fair dinkum – this girl was straight out of a Paul Hogan movie!

'Knock-knock!'

"Hello."

"Can I restock your mini bar?"

"No, I've only been here five minutes and haven't had time to drink any of them yet! Give me half an hour."

'Knock-knock!' (Half an hour later.)

"Can I restock your mini bar now?"

"I was joking!"

"Oh, sorry!"

'Knock-knock!' (Ten minutes later – the first young attendant reappears.)

"Ma'am the hotel would like to offer you an extended checkout service for a fee of $25, which includes $25 credit at the bar and restaurant."

"Thanks, I'll bear that in mind, but as I've only just checked in, I don't need that right now."

'Knock-knock!' (An hour later.)

"House-Keeping!"

"I've just arrived and don't need anything yet."

"I know. Reception asked me to let you know that you only have one towel allocation because we are part of the Green Dream Team."

"Oh, great. I only need one towel."

'Knock-knock!' (A short while later.)

"Ma'am, I thought I'd bring you up this card with the details of the late check-out option."

"How kind. Thank you. Really, I don't need anything except to be left alone." Susanna closed her door.

Thinking about the housekeeping conversation, Susanna was reminded of the time she stayed in a hotel in Cairns. The slogan had read:

We're here to be green.
You know what we mean.
We'll keep you so clean.
Here's a reward from
'The Team!'

The reward had been an offer to receive a $10 refund at checkout if you didn't use the daily house-keeping services. Susanna had availed herself of this reward, but on checkout had received a different message.

"Mrs Newth you only receive a $10 credit voucher for one day, which must be spent the day before in our hotel bar or restaurant."

Susanna had then fetched the advertising information that had clearly stated that a $10 a day refund was offered for each day the client did not use the house-keeping services. Susanna had kept good records, and she had cleaned the apartment herself over the five days of her stay, even washing and drying the towels in the hotel laundry, as well as removing any garbage items.

She felt she was owed this reward!

The receptionist had been flabbergasted. "But we don't do refunds, we only give credit vouchers!"

"But it says here that you do!" Susanna had looked sternly at the lady.

"You need to speak to your manager," was all Susanna had said, as she had smiled kindly at the agitated lady.

On returning, the lady had simply handed the patient Susanna a $50 note, presumably handed to her from the manager. Susanna had graciously accepted, making a mental note to add this hotel to her long list of other hotels she can never stay at again!

Now, turning her attention to the cardboard advertisement handed to her by the young attendant at her current lodgings, she wondered what the fine print of this slogan really meant.

> ***'Not a Morning Person?'***
> ***Enjoy a sleep-in on us!***

"So, what are they offering me?"

At face value the advert offered a late check-out (4pm) for a fee of $25, which included a credit of up to $25 in the bar or restaurant.

"So, what are they really offering me?"

After satisfying herself that this deal seemed good value, she proceeded to reception. Her plane wasn't scheduled to leave until 6pm on the Sunday, so this late check-out time of 4pm would be useful. Plus, the added, bonus of a drinks' credit gave her four free drinks!

When Susanna went to claim her bar credit that night in the bar, she was not surprised when the young bar attendant took the cardboard advertisement out of her hands to read for himself.

"He has never seen one of these before!" Susanna smiled to herself. "Oh, goody! More fun!"

So, Susanna availed herself of the free drinks and thought no more about the matter until check-out.

"Mrs Newth, you have a bar tab of $25. How would you like to pay this, cash or card?"

"Neither!" Susanna smiled at the over-smiling receptionist.

"I don't understand." The less-than-smiling receptionist now peered at her customer.

"I purchased your late check-out option that included a bar credit of up to $25. How are you going to refund my money – cash or card?"

The hotel had taken a $100 bond on check-in, that was due to be refunded at check-out.

"Oh. That doesn't mean you get free drinks at the bar. It means you get up to $25 off if you have a meal in our restaurant after your stay with us has ended."

"But it doesn't say that on this cardboard advertisement!"

"Yes, but that is what we mean!"

"Are you aware that under Australian Consumer Law, you can be fined for false advertising?"

Susanna had felt that this conversation with the receptionist needed to be taken up a notch at this stage. The line of people behind Susanna was beginning to become unsettled at the thought of a lengthy reception wait-time, and the receptionist didn't appear to want to budge on her position.

"I'll just go and consult with my manager."

"Good idea!"

And so it was with no surprise that, on the receptionist's return, Susanna was handed a cash amount of $25. "Mrs Newth you will receive the bond back on you card within three working days."

And so it was, once more, that Susanna left the hotel making a mental note to add this one to her long, growing longer, list of hotels she can never stay at again!

The hotel didn't have to refund her the $25 – they just had to not charge her. They didn't know the intent of their own advertising but had refunded her money because they didn't want a fuss. When will they learn?

Just remember friends,

If you don't want to fight with every hotel receptionist, coffee shop owner, restaurant proprietor or bar attendant, just accept – 'There's no such thing as a free lunch!'

You get what you pay for!

Saga 13
Let Us Reward You!

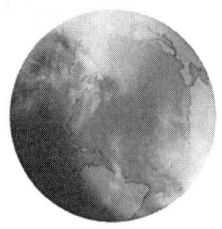

Gosh! Susanna thinks, *All around the globe people are waking up and rushing to their local supermarkets to collect the latest Ooshie, mini supermarket replica, voucher or school sticker – and all for just the small sum spent of $30.*

Susanna is impressed!

"Who are these highly prized, much sought after collectables for?" she asks herself.

She recalls an article last year about a group of middle-aged ladies fighting over one supermarket chain's plastic food replicas – apparently, they wanted to trade duplicates for ones they hadn't received. They had been annoyed at not being able to do so.

"Do these people have nothing else to do? What do these items do? Where do they keep them? What is their purpose?"

These are rhetorical questions that Susanna knows full well the answers to. She wonders, though, if the latest 'reward' on offer from one supermarket chain, will have quite the same appeal as the cute little Lion King toys. She is not sure the miniscule little packets of three vegetable seeds will entice children sufficiently to nag their parents to spend $30, just so they can collect these little treasures.

"Are the big supermarket chains so concerned about losing customers, that they feel they have to 'reward' them with toys or other enticements?" Susanna ponders. Apparently, they do, because as soon as one company begins a campaign the rival chain also begins a similar one. When that campaign finishes, you can expect the other one to end as well – and of course, the amount of dollars consumers must spend to receive such a reward from either chain is – exactly the same!

Susanna certainly remembers the enormous fuss both these companies made about not providing plastic bags anymore. For years, previously, both supermarket chains had informed customers that they were planning to end supplying free plastic bags to customers, and instead began producing better quality re-usable ones at a notional price. At first, people began purchasing these canvas or plastic alternatives but soon fell foul of actually bringing them shopping with them.

"How can people be so lazy?" Susanna squirms in horror.

This laziness, though, soon saw people leaving these bags at home and using them for other purposes, while they continued to use the free plastic ones as they had done before. People simply said, "Why buy bags when they give them to us for free?"

In 2018, however, Susanna became excited! Yes, she actually thought the big supermarket chains had finally become serious about 'The Environment Debate'!

As Susanna knows, it's not the bags that are really the problem, it's the way people discard them that causes the big issues.

These bags were very light and easily became blown to the winds, eventually ending up in storm water drains or the oceans – becoming highly hazardous to marine creatures.

"Gosh! They have even given customers a deadline by which they must organise their own bags!"

Two weeks later…

"So, nothing changes then?" she grimaces. "They can't resist! They are so fearful of losing any customers, that they have now provided a few million plastic bags – just in case anyone has forgotten to bring the ones they were told to bring."

Susanna shakes her head in shame at people's laziness once again. She also shakes her head again at the fuss the customers made at now having to pay a small fee of 15c per bag! (This was the compromise both supermarket chains came up with. Better quality plastic bags at a price!)

"So, do we really care about the environment? No, of course not! What are these little Ooshies and mini supermarket collectables made from? Plastic, inside plastic put into plastic bags to carry home." Susanna shakes her head again in disbelief.

Ah, she recently reads an article in which Consumer Watch castigates both supermarket chains for their continued use and abuse of plastic.

"Ah, so what is the latest fad? Plant seeds.

"And in what type of container do these seeds come in?"

"Plastic!"

Addendum

Susanna has just read an article in a local news outlet informing the general public that their supermarkets will soon be bringing back paper bags. Are these any better for the environment?

Yes, on the one hand paper certainly breaks down and can be recycled more readily, but is it better for the environment?

Here is some information – you decide!

- Paper bags are not as durable and so not reusable.
- Paper bags are bulkier and so require greater quantities of transportation in order for waste to be taken to recycling centres – this creates far more greenhouse emissions (7 truckloads for 2 million bags as compared to 1 truck load for 2 million plastic ones).
- Paper bags require 4 times more water in order to be produced and in the process generate 3 times more greenhouse gases.
- Paper bags, in their production, consume 2.2 times more renewable energy and 2.7 times more acid gases than in the plastic bag production.

Do We Really Care?

Do We Really Care?

Paper or plastic, cotton or elastic, bits and bobs and saws galore are fuel for bins or rubbish tins when we don't want them anymore.

Does it really matter if we all get fatter? Bags of chips with sauce galore are fuel we need when time to feed until our stomachs take no more.

Which does baby prefer - a soft, cotton nappy soaked in bleach for hours galore in plastic bins with fitted lids so we can't smell them anymore?

Or little paper ones that fit on bums discarded, when wee wees done, in plastic tins or rubbish bins so they can't use them anymore.

Is the water purer from the springs at Leura? Twist and sip these droplets cold that flood your veins like icy rains and leave you feeling wanting more.

What's wrong with tap water for your son and daughter? Turn the tap for stores galore, it's always cold with never mould and leaves your healthy evermore.

Gosh, now this has got me thinking, Susanna thinks. "Is paper better than plastic?"

Susanna recalls the time when the palliative care nurses would visit her sick husband every day to bring supplies and do treatments, always bringing with them a large paper bag. Into this bag would then be placed an assortment of paper and plastic scraps, syringes, cream containers and other assorted detritus. The bag would be bulging by the end of the visit and Susanna would be requested to dispose of 'the bag'.

She had asked a nurse one day, "Why do you use paper bags?"

"Because it's better for the environment?" had come her terse and very snappy retort.

Mulling this over, Susanna couldn't help but look puzzled. Did her statement imply that paper was good for the environment? Both paper and plastic are bad – they both create emissions that are toxic to our beautiful planet.

"Have we lost the plot?" she worries. "If the health profession – on mass – across Australia – conforms to these practices – just think how much paper trash (as well as plastic scraps) go to landfill every day." Susanna shakes her head in shame.

Susanna also shakes her head again at the thought of how many paper bags large take away food companies consume every day. She was once involved in a survey of how many paper cups a juice outlet used in a busy lunch hour – a staggering 800 large cups for milkshakes or juices, 680 medium cups for freshly squeezed fruit juices and 130 small cups for their gelato smoothies. (Most customers discarded their cups in the bins provided at the shop. These cups were collected in large, black plastic bags and tipped into the regular garbage – none were recycled!)

Susanna smiles. She is a minimalist! She only eats vegetables and drinks sparkly white wine or green tea (the occasional decaffeinated black coffee), owns a very small wardrobe of clothes and recycles as much as she can each week.

She is an avid supporter of charity shops, always donating any unwanted items or used clothing – always in excellent condition to her nearest outlet, so that they can be recycled for others to use, as well as generate funds for the organisation.

"Nah. I'll give these a miss!"

Good for you, Susanna! So, you won't be rushing to grab the environmentally friendly green seeds in their little plastic bags from your local supermarket?

Saga 14
The Unwelcome Guest

It was twelve months after her husband had passed away that Susanna decided it might be fun to have a house mate. Living alone in a three-bedroomed unit can be lonesome, even though she always kept busy. So, she advertised…

Now, who would not want to move in with Susanna?

Hey, darlin'
I'm your perfect flatmate. I'm clean, tidy, like a beer – or two, have little washing and enjoy the company of blokes – so I'll be at the pub most nights!
Trevor
Tradie by trade!

This little note from Trevor is 'fair dinkum!' (Just the name has been changed for privacy reasons).

Susanna also received many other offers from various others to share her modest townhouse accommodation. However, hard as it was to choose, she declined Trevor's offer, as she had only advertised for females, and Trevor didn't qualify on that count. She's not sure he understood that, though, as he persisted with his offer for several weeks. (Perhaps other potential landlords also preferred not to rent their rooms to the tradie set who resided with their boyfriends, because poor Trevor became quite desperate for somewhere to live!)

Susanna, open-minded and liberal as she always is, was more concerned about the muddy boots, cement dust and heavy overalls to be washed daily, than she was about the man's sexual preferences, decided politely against inviting him to rent the beautifully furnished queen bedroom with ensuite, walk in robes and wall to wall white, plush carpet, ceiling fan and R/C Air – Con; open lounge with polished timber floors, Smart flat-screen TV including Netflix, leather lounges; separate kitchen with stainless-steel gas appliances, fridge and dishwasher; internal laundry – including dryer; double garage and large downstairs study, plus spacious covered patio with dining table, umbrella, patio blinds and outdoor heater. Gas heating up and down and utilities included in the modest rent.

(*Was it the 'modest' rent that attracted so many prospective renters?* Susanna wondered!)

And, so it was, that Trevor went his own happy way and Susanna offered the room to Lucy, a 41-year-old lady who worked locally.

Susanna reflects five weeks later – sometimes a situation can be soooo outrageously bad that it becomes funny!

So, what went wrong?

At first Lucy enjoyed Susanna's hospitality, coming home and helping herself to the assortments of delicious pastas, casseroles, stir fries, or noodle and vegetable dishes waiting in the fridge, and then helping herself to one of dozens of little bottles of special Champagne, usually only reserved for Susanna, and sitting back to watch her choice of Netflix on the big screen with a caramel fudge in one hand and one of Susanna's son's coveted double-chocked ice-creams in the other. Yes, she thought, she had struck it rich!

Lucy was like the cat that had got the cream!

Well, rich it was when Susanna smiled a friendly smile to the lady as Susanna trekked off to Brisbane for a long weekend and offered Lucy the option to enjoy her hospitality during her absence over the weekend.

And even richer it became when Susanna returned at midnight on the Sunday night to find all the external and internal lights left on and Lucy nowhere to be seen. When challenged about this the next day, on returning from wherever she had been, had simply said, "Yes, that was me!"

And, rich it was when Susanna later discovered the lady had moved her boyfriend in for the weekend – only evacuating the premises an hour before Susanna had arrived home on the Sunday night – during which time the pair had set up cameras all around the house.

Going to bed on the Monday night after her wonderful weekend away, Susanna had been tired. Her little, modest downstairs quarters are not as luxuriant as the upstairs option, but they are adequate for the lone lady, who has simple needs and likes the quiet life. She has a comfortable bed and a small TV. That night, though, she was too tired to watch her favourite shows and slept easily.

On waking at her usual hour of 3am. she ventured quietly upstairs to make the first of her special brews for the day, always changing the coffee pot water and cleaning the pod container to ensure the coffee brewed to its maximum flavour and potential.

Yes, this first coffee of the day is simply divine!

Just the thought of the coffee's wonderful aroma is usually enough to set Susanna into a calm and relaxed mood for the day. But, she was anything but calm as she ventured upstairs to discover every single upstairs light had been left on as high at it could possibly go.

What's going on? she had thought. This is a deliberate message – not on! Not having it! No way!

Making her coffee, turning all lights off, and then venturing back to the privacy of her own space, Susanna was left wondering what lady Lucy was up to!

With cameras now secretly installed around the internal sections of the house, Lucy was able to monitor her landlady's movements. These movements, Susanna contemplates, must have made for a somewhat uninteresting morning for her. Her working schedules are mundane and predictable to say the least.

Susanna writes, prepares her lessons and finishes in time for her afternoon teaching programs.

On this next day, the Tuesday, Lucy remained locked in her room, away from any accountability of explaining her actions to her host, until she took herself off to an exercise class. Susanna then did not set eyes on her again until later that night.

One would have thought a freight train had hurtled through the house as Lucy thundered up the stairs at this late hour. Carrying several heavy items of baggage, she had scraped all the paintwork on her journey upwards, glaring angrily – no – more angrily than I can describe – there are no words to describe the horribly hostile manner in which this lady entered the premises that night!

Susanna had just sat down to enjoy her dinner, when the lady had disturbed this quiet, end of the day moment. Feeling somewhat annoyed by Lucy's behaviour, Susanna had quietly said, "Lucy, what is the matter?"

Susanna was not expecting the response…

As she had stared open-mouthed at the anger, hostility, physical aggression and immense anxiety that was oozing out of every pore in this lady's body, she had calmly retorted, "I have been nothing but kind, helpful and generous to you. You have a few problems – don't deflect blame for those onto me. Thank you for spoiling my dinner and evening."

The kind host had then walked downstairs to her room. She did not sleep that night.

"This lady has more than a few screws loose!" Susanna could only shake her head in bewilderment. "Wow, I never saw that coming!"

The next day started as the Tuesday had. Lucy was not offered much work this week, which is one of the reasons Susanna thinks is the cause of her sudden change in mood. (Does she think Susanna is responsible for her not being offered any shifts?

No, Susanna had no claim to any reason why her guest had suddenly become so outwardly and aggressively angry towards her. She had simply gone to Brisbane and returned home. Everything had been fine before she had left, and on her return the situation had become chaotic and unacceptable.

It had been noon when Susanna had first heard signs of life upstairs. The lady had busied herself until such time as she decided to leave for the day, turning all lights on upstairs and leaving the front door and garage doors wide open in an unsecured and unsafe manner.

It had been fortunate that Susanna had still been at home and could rectify the situation immediately. Such was not the case the next day. Susanna had broken her routine on this day to attend at her accountant's premises to complete her tax return. It had been Susanna's neighbour, who had phoned her at noon to let her know the house was wide open and all the lights were on – internal and external. Susanna had asked her neighbour to switch all the lights off and secure her house – her neighbour has keys to her house, for such emergencies. Susanna and her friend have reciprocal arrangements.

On finding out about this complete lack of respect for Susanna's property, careless disregard for any house rules and total disregard for any responsibility towards Susanna or her house, Susanna messaged the errant lady later that day.

Once again Susanna does not disclose the intricate details of the written messages that were relayed that day, as this serves no useful purpose. The only comment that Lucy was able to define about her current disposition was to say, "Don't smother me with your kindness as bribery for wanting me to be your friend – no wonder you have no friends!"

Well, Susanna does have friends – she may joke a little in her sagas that she prefers not to become too socially involved with them, but she has always communicated amiably with her fellow colleagues, family and close-knit 'winos' – friends who share this common pastime!

It was somewhere around the fifteenth message when Susanna realised enough was enough and notified the corresponding partner that she was terminating the rental agreement due to her unacceptable behaviour. In the final wash, there had been over 30 pages of offensive emails written to Susanna that afternoon, of which Susanna had only responded to two of them – one that notified Lucy of the termination and one that notified her of Susanna's intentions.

When Susanna returned home that night around 4.30pm the bird had flown!

Yes, she had spat the dummy! Yes, she had stolen food! Yes, she had left a mess! Yes, she had left garbage all around the house and even one heavy chair on Susanna's front lawn. Yes, she had left bags half-packed in her room and yes, all the lights were blazing, and all external doors were left open.

No, no keys had been returned.

When Susanna had requested to Lucy that she be permitted to enter her room to switch off the lights, Lucy had vehemently replied, "NO!"

Fine, Susanna had thought. *So be it!*

It had been midday the following Saturday when loud banging of doors, car doors slamming and raised, argumentative voices suddenly invaded Susanna's quiet, homely premises. As the writer worked in her study, she could discern two adults making an assault on all upstairs areas of the house. They were in and out in less than five minutes, once more leaving all lights on and all external doors wide open.

When Susanna went to inspect rooms upstairs, she felt a huge weight lift off her shoulders. Sighing a heavy sigh, she had smiled, "She's gone!"

Susanna had then – cleaned up! She had her house back.

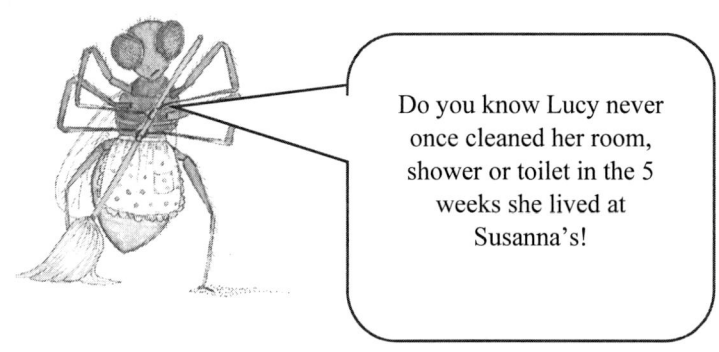

Do you know Lucy never once cleaned her room, shower or toilet in the 5 weeks she lived at Susanna's!

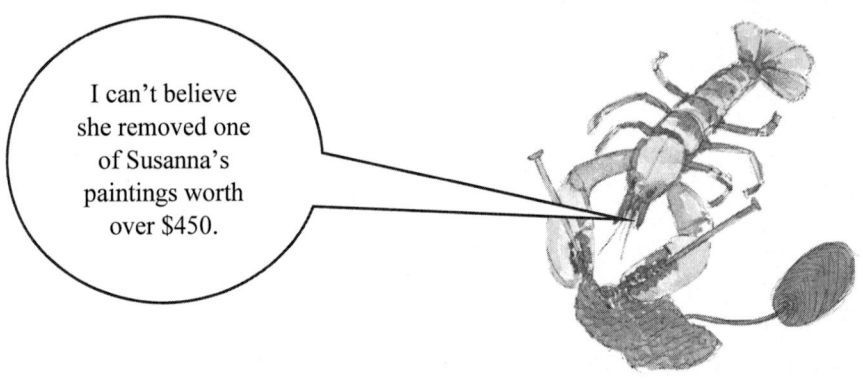

Police officers had been notified and a report was filed. The officers also assisted Susanna to locate the painting.

Susanna always asks the rhetorical question, "Why do people who do the wrong thing always blame those who do the right thing?"

She was gone.

And, of course, she owed money!

Did she think Susanna had 'money to burn'!

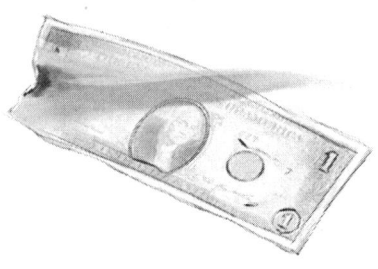

Saga 15
Those Magic Words

> Most of Susanna's sagas are born in the everyday mishaps that happen. She never knows what each new week will bring, or where each new saga will take her. The first part of this saga is an amusing memory of a time she and her husband had enjoyed a lunch out near the beach one Sunday, and Susanna had sent back her garden salad five times. The lady who had made the salad at no time had accepted that she was at fault.
> The middle section of the saga outlines a couple of other occasions when Susanna encountered people who did the wrong thing, but once again refused to accept any liability for their wrongdoing.
> The closing section is a quick flick into the diet and exercise question.

"Can we go for coffee?"

Ah, those magic words I would hear when the sun was shining outside, and the husband just wanted to spend time with his wife sitting in a café on the beach.

(Well, he really wants the coffee – no, actually he really wants the cake that comes with the coffee – well, no – the cake doesn't come with the coffee, but he will buy one anyway, well, no – **he** won't, but his wife **will** buy him one!)

The cake must be just right – not too sweet, not too big, not too cakie and not too creamy. It must not be mushy or sloshy and yet not be hard and crunchy. The most favoured little cakie is a Neenish tart, or possibly a Bakewell, or even a Manchester one that has the custard. When he lived in England, he soooo looooved his Eccles cakes – these are flaky pastries with raisins inside.

His wife – well, she doesn't eat cakes. She doesn't particularly like sweet foods and cannot eat anything that contains fats of any kind. The thought of a buttery butter-cake or pound slice with icing, would send her into a giddy spin. So, she declines gracefully.

Going to any café or restaurant, to indulge in a favourite recipe, is not on Susanna's top ten list of things to do. The reason for this is that there is no favourite recipe that Susanna cooks at home, and certainly not one found in any restaurant. Sitting writing this saga, she is reminded of the occasion when she sent back a garden salad five times. On the sixth time, the salad was literally 'thrown' at her by the proprietor, who had said, "Madam, here is your tossed salad – I made it myself!"

Susanna still laughs at the look on the lady's face, as well as the obvious pun she had made – that, of course, she had, had no idea she had made (tossed!) Yes, the salad was well and truly 'tossed'! She had enjoyed it – and she hadn't paid for it – and she'd managed to get a free glass of wine as well!

Susanna and Michael had been sitting in a largish Italian restaurant overlooking Northbeach in Wollongong one warm and lazy Sunday afternoon. The kitchen area was part of the open food preparation space, and so the two ladies preparing the salads were visible as they cut up the vegetables. Susanna didn't need to see what they were doing to know what they were doing wrong, but she could see the look on one lady's face every time a salad was returned to her.

"Why is it that when people do the wrong thing, they always blame others?"

This question will be considered again, later in this saga and probably in many later ones too!

The lady preparing the salad had lazily not washed the colander each time she had prepared a salad, leaving traces of oil on Susanna's leaves. Even the slightest trace can cause a problem for her, as the husband well knew.

The first time: "Excuse me, but the lady has put oil on my salad, and I asked for one without any oil."

"Ma'am, she says it is only a bit of Balsamic dressing."

"That's oil," Susanna smiles at the waiter, as she hands him her freshly made and quite untouched salad.

The second time: "Excuse me, but the lady has added something to the lettuce, and I asked for nothing to be added."

"She has put some lemon juice dressing on the leaves to make it taste better for you."

"But I didn't ask for it," Susanna again smiles, as she hands him back her second freshly made salad.

The third time: "Excuse me, but there is a glaze on the leaves. I cannot eat this."

"Ma'am the lady who prepared your salad said she hasn't put anything on the leaves."

"Yes, she has. Look." The waiter looks perplexed at her freshly made, untouched salad, as does everyone else in the restaurant by this time. Susanna is fast becoming the entertainment of the afternoon!

The lady who is preparing Susanna's salads by this time, too, is becoming extremely agitated and keeps giving Susanna glaring glances.

Hello, Susanna thinks, *is she blaming me for her wrong-doing?*

The fourth time: "Excuse me, but the lady has done the same thing again!" Susanna's voice this time reflecting a slight edge to it.

No comment from the waiter, who simply takes the bowl of freshly made garden salad and places it under the nose of the lady who is by now, opening sneering at Susanna. Everyone in the restaurant watches with eager eyes and ears at what both she and Susanna are going to do next!

Susanna's husband, usually not a supporter of his wife's disagreements with the many and varied establishments she frequently ends up disagreeing with, remains calm and non-committal on this occasion. (He knows his wife will become unwell if she eats the food she has been given. He is as much annoyed as Susanna is, that the restaurant just can't get it right!)

The fifth time: "Excuse me, can you please tell the lady to just wash the vegetables in cold water and put them on a plate. It's what I asked you to do the first time I ordered this garden salad. What she is doing is placing them in a colander that has contained oil, which then washes onto my freshly washed green leaves. Please take this away and bring me a glass of wine instead. I've given up on the garden salad."

Susanna cannot say how many times she has sat in restaurants and just sipped wine. She likes wine. She especially likes very cold, very dry, very sparkling and very fruity white wine.

The young man brings Susanna the wine she has asked for, every eye and breath in the restaurant freezing in time as he hands it to her.

"Delicious, thank you," as Susanna takes her first sip.

"Madam, here is your garden salad – I made it myself," every eye and breath still on tenterhooks, keenly watching the proprietor as she hands Susanna the bowl of freshly made garden salad.

> *It was at the exact moment that Susanna placed a fork in the lettuce, speared it and placed it into her mouth, that the entire audience of eaters erupted into a frenzied applause. The proprietor had then walked away embarrassed, the lady who had prepared the first five salads scowled openly at Susanna and the husband joined in the embarrassment of the proprietor.*

Susanna had said to him, "At what point was any of that charade – my fault?" Michael had just shaken, his head.

The fellow luncheoners that day hadn't thought it was Susanna's fault. However, they had been intrigued as to why the salad hadn't been suitable each time, and they were certainly amazed that anyone would have the gall to send back food once – let alone five times! Still it had been entertainment they weren't expecting!

So, the rhetorical question once again – why do people who do the wrong thing always blame **others** for their wrong-doing?

The Lazy Driver

"Lady, you're in my way!" a very rude and rather large gentleman driving a work vehicle yells at Susanna, as she attempts to drive out of her local petrol station recently. She is on her way to work and is running a little late.

"Actually, you're in my way!" Susanna opens her side window and smiles pleasantly at him.

"Yeah, love, but my truck is bigger than your car, so **you** need to move!" he growls back at Susanna.

"But, why should **I** move, when **you've** done the wrong thing?" Susanna now glares her retort back at him, a little less patiently than the first time.

"Sir, you've driven the wrong way down a one-way street that I now need to go the right way down. It's your laziness that has caught you in this mess." Susanna glares back at him.

Having no choice, except to accommodate the man's needs, Susanna reverses her car to allow him to drive in. She then thinks, *At no time does he think he has done anything wrong!*

The Selfish Neighbour

"Hello, you can't park your vehicle in that spot, as it's reserved for disability access vehicles only." Susanna approaches a lady who has parked her car in this spot every day for 3 months. The lady is Susanna's neighbour. When she goes to work at 8am she parks her car in the disabled parking and then travels to work with a co-worker, leaving her car there all day.

"Why don't you park your car in your garage like everyone else?" Susanna pleasantly asks her.

"And why don't you mind your own business!" came the very rude and abusively snorted retort.

"Because you've done the wrong thing – not me!" Susanna firmly glares at her neighbour. "Today I need to use this space. I have a very large disabled Maxi vehicle coming into this site and need somewhere it can park. As this space is designated especially for this purpose, I am asking you to move your vehicle."

The lady continues to glare at Susanna, as she slams the car doors shut loudly and then drives off to work with her co-worker, not giving a second thought to the situation.

Susanna shakes her head, as she is left to find alternative parking for the Maxi taxi.

On returning home from work that night, the neighbour leaves a rather rude-looking cactus plant in the porch of Susanna's house. At first, Susanna thinks it has been left as a gift, but quickly realises it is a practical joke – a symbolic gesture, when she sees her neighbour sneaking into Susanna's porch to retrieve it a short while later. (Susanna had been disappointed – she had quite liked the cactus and would have eagerly placed it with her collection of plants on her patio.)

As a result of the lady's unlawful parking breach, the Strata Corporation had then issued her with a Breach Notice that carried a fine of $1000.

And so, it was that the next day, returning from work, Susanna found all her garden beds vandalised – all the plants had been chopped up with scissors and left at the side of each flower bed. The police report estimation of damage was $1000.

Well, well, well!

Let's look at the title of this saga! 'Those Magic Words' – apart from the deliciously-sounding coffee ones, another set of little words that always amuses Susanna is, "I'm on a diet."

Are people really on diets, or is this just an excuse? What do people really, mean by these five little words?

Fight the Flab

Susanna was left wondering this last week when a staff member at her work, when asked if she would like some cheese, strawberries and crackers, had smiled and said, "No, I'm on a diet."

Susanna had thought, *Fine.*

The next day, Susanna had passed the same teacher's table and noticed some tell-tale chocolate wrappers left carelessly beside that teacher's lesson books.

"So, she's not on a diet… she's on a chocolate diet… she's only on a non-cheese, strawberries and crackers diet…?"

Susanna knows too well the answers to these questions. It's the same conundrum that arouses her interests when people decide to join fitness centres. Do they join these establishments to get fit? Do they join to lose weight? Do people have to lose weight to get fit – or do they think they have to lose weight to be fit? Can one put on weight and still get fit? Is losing weight being fitter? Does exercising **more** lead to losing weight?

This diet debate has been around for Susanna's entire life. She recalls elderly ladies complaining to her mother that they had better not have a second piece of chocolate cake being offered them, because they are 'watching their weight.'

Susanna had thought, *Yes, they certainly are watching their weight when they see themselves getting fatter after eating their third slice of chocolate cake! Why can't they be satisfied with only one slice? Better still, why can't they just say 'no'. Do they really, want it?*

Susanna is a member of a fitness centre – a multi-purpose centre that boasts two swimming pools and the usual assortments of exercise machines and classes. Susanna likes to swim. She also likes to road run. Her fitness centre is her fun – she has friends there and she enjoys a coffee after her workout.

Does she meet her fitness goals? No, because she doesn't set any! *Does anyone?* she thinks as she surveys the mottled crew of people from all walks of life who have just joined her in the café for a coffee.

"The 'oldies' set clearly come for the social life! They've steadily put on weight since I've known them. I've watched them walking slowly up and down the pool for the last hour exercising their tongues more than their bodies. Now they'll order their schnitzel burgers with the lot – rewards for their efforts!" Susanna smiles.

"Coffee anyone?"

Saga 16
The English Teacher

> The next saga Susanna would like to share is when she was working as a high school teacher. She has since retired from full-time teaching, but eagerly watches the new batches of teachers head off to their first appointments on Day 1 of Term 1 each year.

How Susanna enjoys watching all the newly trained, eager beavers heading off to their first assignments as new recruits in the public education system on their first day of the new school year. She wonders how many of them will last the distance, as she had done – her stint of fifty years as a specialist subject teacher, senior education officer and finally principal of three schools – two at the same time, held memories to make her smile for a lifetime.

She wondered if the young gentlemen, so brash and brazen, would be wearing their freshly – ironed business shirts with ties and suits, the following day! She suspected not – yes, they were all quick learners. (That's why they became teachers!)

As she reflects on her memories, she admits she could write a plethora of sagas, but deigns only to write this one for her many followers of her stories. She wonders too, if people who are not teachers fully appreciate the difficulties teachers encounter in their attempts to provide education to students, who only see school as a somewhat rude interruption to their social lives.

One mother had phoned Susanna one morning around 8am. "Mrs Newth can you please tell me why my daughter has just spent two hours getting ready for her day at school?"

"No. Did you ask her?"

The lady had become frustrated that her Year 8 daughter only saw school as a social gathering, having lost all interest in all things educational.

"Can I ask you why you're asking me this question?"

"Because you have her for English!" the even more frustrated mother had then yelled down the phone, as she became even more frustrated by Susanna's seemingly uncaring and terse responses to her problem.

Yes, Susanna smiled as she recalls calming the mother and reassuring her that her daughter was actually, doing quite well in Susanna's class, and that there was no need for concern.

She again muses to herself why the mother chose to speak to her daughter's English teacher and not the somewhat ageing, soon to be retired, Mathematics teacher. Of c ourse, Susanna knew that answer!

(No parent ever chose to speak with 'Gazza' on the phone, and even fewer ventured to his desk on parent/teacher nights.)

So, why was Susanna teaching English? Good question!

"Mrs Newth, can I please speak to you in my office?"

Susanna had been casually walking away from the staff room, when the newly appointed principal had approached her. Gauging that Susanna wasn't really being given a choice, she smiled pleasantly at the lady, nodded and followed her into her office.

"Mrs Newth, I'm the new principal. It's nice to meet you."

The two had shaken hands and seated themselves comfortably in readiness for their chat.

"Did you know there's another Newth on staff?"

"Er… Yes. Our paths cross occasionally…we've both been here for 20 years – I can't avoid him really – he's my husband!"

Susanna thinks, *Did she seriously just ask me that question?*

"Oh, Sue, you're so funny!" the large lady had smiled broadly at her PE teacher.

"Sue, I want you to teach English to Year 8 this year."

"Why?"

"Why not?"

"Because I'm not employed here as an English teacher."

"You're English!"

"Yes, but I'm not an English teacher!"

"Sue, I've heard on the grapevine that you're very, very good at English!" the smile this time was glassy, fake and forceful in a way that Susanna knew she had no escape. An English teacher she was to be for that year.

Fronting up for her first class, the following day, Susanna quickly surmised the reason why she had been especially chosen to teach English to this designated English 6 class. Of the six English classes in Year 8, the other five all had specialist English teachers – trained to teach English – all of which contained enthusiastic and capable students!

Now, Susanna has no problem teaching anything to anyone. She enjoys teaching. She is good at it. The students knew her well and were not unreceptive to accepting her as their English teacher for the year. However, when students are placed in graded classes, one feels a little sorry for the students who end up in the bottom group. (Well, Susanna does!) It affects their self-esteem, motivation and willingness to participate in lessons.

Needless to say, Susanna set about providing her class with a stimulating and enjoyable English curriculum. As she reflects on these lessons, she smiles as she recalls some of her methods for classroom management. Susanna still smiles to this day, as she recalls this lesson.

It was a Tuesday afternoon, just after lunch, when three girls entered Susanna's classroom half-way through the lesson.

"Do you have late notes?" their teacher looks at them sternly.

The three girls respond by giggling, seating themselves in the back row and facing the back wall.

Susanna continues the lesson. The girls continue to giggle and keep their backs facing Susanna.

After allowing the girls a few minutes of self – expression to see how far they were going to go with their little prank, Susanna quietly says, "Kathryn, I'm playing squash at home tonight!"

Of course, the ardent and very skilled classroom practitioner knows exactly how to manage this situation, and how those few simple words would send the errant Kathryn (the ring leader) into a fitful spin, instantly spinning around the trio to face the front, sit bolt upright, take out their books and begin their lesson, paying avid attention to their English teacher.

So, how was it that those magic words so magically worked?

Susanna played competition squash for the local fitness centre near the school. When her team played at home, they co-shared the centre with the same graded male team, of which Kathryn's father was a player. Playing at home would mean Susanna would be spending the evening chatting to Kathryn's dad!

"Yes, good decision girl!" Susanna had smirked to herself.

When the three girls had settled and keenly eying their teacher, she had quietly said, without looking up from her desk, "Now you three girls are to write a statement outlining what you have been doing since this lesson began."

She had then looked up and stared sternly at their frozen faces.

Handing in their statements, Susanna had then spoken to the three students about their behaviour, once the other students had left the room.

"If you choose to behave in that way again, these statements will be sent home to your parents. Do we understand each other?"

The girls had nodded, as they took the late notes Susanna had provided them with, so that they were covered for their next lesson.

Had Susanna shown anger towards these girls on their entry into class that day, the girls would have been openly rude and abusive back to their teacher – she knew this – she had witnessed them behaving that way to other teachers on many occasions. Had she castigated them in front of the class, it would have given the power to the students, particularly when they had formed a group, and even more so when the ringleader controlled every student in the class.

Yes, Susanna had studied educational psychology. Susanna had known this situation called for one of her many 'tricks' that she kept up her sleeve, for just such occasions! Sitting watching the sea as she sits sipping her delicious afternoon green tea on her patio, Susanna also smiles to herself as she remembers the ensuing scenario that occurred a short while after the final school bell had rung for that day. Susanna had done her banking and was returning to her car.

"Hello Mrs Newth," a smiling lady had rushed up to intercept Susanna. "Kathryn was just telling me how much she enjoys her English lessons with you!"

Now, Susanna, always one to play 'the game'!

"Oh, yes, Mrs Willoughby. You have no idea how much your daughter enjoys her lessons. She enjoys them so much she always makes sure she is the first student in the room and the last to leave."

Kathryn, hiding behind her mother's large, shopping bags, cringes and squirms, desperately hoping her teacher will not divulge any comment about their lesson today. To avoid any such comment, the very clever and cunning teenager quickly joins in Susanna's game.

"Oh, Mum, we are so fortunate to have Mrs Newth. She is the 'best' teacher. I know I'm going to do really well in English this year."

Susanna smiles at her artful student but does not for one second believe a word that has erupted from the girl's mouth. Susanna may have been allocated the lowest of the English classes to teach, but every student in her class was a very capable and talented student in many areas of English.

As Susanna reflects on the trio of girls who had exploded into her classroom on that occasion, she recalls that one of the girls later went on to become extremely famous as a member of the cast of Home and Away, a role the girl played for many years.

"Well, Kathryn, you certainly have the ability to do well, and I'm going to personally make sure that you get plenty of study practice. I'll prepare a special English workbook for you to do at home."

Susanna had then said her farewells to the smiling pair and headed off to her car. The next day in class, Kathryn had approached Susanna to thank her for keeping quiet about their stupid prank.

"Mrs Newth, you're not really going to give me extra homework, are you?"

"No, of course not!"

The girl had breathed a sigh of relief. "You know, you really are the best!"

"Yeah, I know! Just don't mess with me again!"

At the end of the year, the principal had approached Susanna and simply said, "Sue, I hear you enjoyed teaching English to Year 8."

"Of course, Principal," Susanna had smiled. "But don't give them to me again!"

Saga 17
Fair Cop – or Not!

> The next set of sagas are about everyday situations that everyone experiences. Some situations make us feel annoyed, whilst others incite a much stronger response. Instead of becoming openly angry or aggrieved by the mistakes or errors of others, Susanna prefers to exercise her pen on paper.

In life Susanna accepts that good things happen as well as bad, that sometimes it's our fault, and sometimes it's not – and that at times we may be blamed for things that are not our fault. *Yeah, we balance it out,* she thinks.

"Are we ever given credit for things we haven't done but have thought to have done?" she asks herself. "No, I don't think so, but I have certainly worn blame for others' wrong-doing," she grimaces.

An incident comes to mind. Susanna used to race across the roads and highways in Sydney north to south – east to west in setting up literacy programs in schools to demonstrate strategies for teaching students with reading difficulties. She enjoyed her work, as well as the freedom it afforded her in being on the road during school hours.

It had been a Wednesday morning. She had picked up her teaching assistant and was travelling to a local high school about seven kilometres away. Driving along she had been amused that the car immediately ahead of hers was an identical make, model and colour. There had been no one else on that stretch of road at the time, and Raina, Susanna's assistant, had smiled, "We're twins driving along!"

Nodding, Susanna had agreed. *The difference is,* she thinks to herself, *they're speeding*!

Suddenly in the mirror, Susanna sees a police car blazing behind her, all lights flashing and a beeping sound requesting her to pull over. At first, Susanna had expected the police car to pass her and head off in search of the errant car in front of hers that had been speeding, but she soon realised the police officers were asking her to stop, and were becoming a little annoyed by her non-compliance.

She pulls over and winds down her window.

"Driver's licence," is all one of the officers says. An offsider, loitering behind his partner, glares disinterestedly at the two ladies in the front seats.

"Badges," Susanna smiles at the first one, and then at the loiterer, who at this unusual request begins to show a little more interest in the two front-seated ladies.

"I asked you first!" the first police officer snarled at Susanna.

"And I'd like to record your badge numbers – first!" Susanna then picks up a nearby pad and pen she always carries in her car for such purposes and waits patiently.

"Madam, can you please step out of the car," the police officer by now becoming openly annoyed, sneering leeringly at the lady three times his senior.

"Officer, I'm not going to ask you again. If you cannot show me your badges, I will close my window and phone the Police Assistance Line."

The loiterer, at this implicitly stated threat, suddenly shakes off his boorish attitude, stands to attention and smiles bemusedly at his senior partner. *Yes,* he thinks, *this day is suddenly becoming surprisingly interesting.*

Within a few seconds both officers present Susanna with their badges – one sneering and one smiling at her. Having noted their details in her notebook, Susanna hands the first officer her licence and begins to exit the car.

"No, stay there!" the aggrieved officer stares sternly at his defiant customer. "Are you aware of the reason I've asked you to pull over?"

"No."

"Madam, you were doing 77 in a 60 zone."

"Ah," Susanna suddenly realises, as she turns to her assistant. "He's mistaken us for the four boys who were ahead of us."

Hearing the ladies' conversation, the police officer looks at his assistant. An arrogance about the man, though, prohibits him from admitting he's made a mistake. It's quite clear he doesn't want Susanna to win this fight and so continues his aggressive stance towards her. Checking her licence and car registration, he saunters back to her waiting car and writes her out a ticket.

"Officer," Susanna's teaching assistant now leans over to the front driver's window. "My husband is the police commissioner at (she gives his location and name) and I'm witness to Susanna driving at 58 kilometres. She has a speedo notification on her dashboard," Raina laughs at the man. "I can see her speed at all times. You should have stopped the boys in the car in front."

At this unexpected light on the situation, the two police officers hastily head back to their car and hope to hear no more about the incident. Of course, they do! Raina made sure of that! Susanna would have taken the bad – accepting there have been times when she has been speeding and not been booked. But…not to be on this occasion.

At the end of their teaching session at the school, Raina had phoned her husband to complain about the incident.

"Yes, it certainly helps to have friends (or family members) in high places," Susanna smiles. How she loves these little tricky incidents that most people find stressful. She knows her rights and she is never afraid to exert them – albeit in quiet, respectful ways. Susanna knows the secret is to always stay calm, smile pleasantly and speak only what is absolutely necessary.

And so it was that later on that afternoon, when Susanna and Raina sat sipping tea in the police commissioner's office, the two young police officers entered to offer their apologies. And, of course, Susanna, gracious as always – accepted them.

That night, after returning home, Susanna is reminded of another incident that involved her having to deal with police matters within her professional capacity.

It had been a few years earlier, when she had been working as a teacher in a high school. Once again it was a Wednesday, but a little later in the day. Susanna was out on the back, playing field with a group of students engaged in a sport session.

Hearing the loud throttling sounds of a car engine revving to maximum power, Susanna and her students had looked up immediately. They had then all fled for their lives as the car, along with its four naked occupants, began careering into the centre of their teaching space, chasing students all around the oval.

Susanna had yelled at some girls, "Hide behind the seats," and at others, "Get the office to phone the police!"

For several minutes the four boys enjoyed yelling obscenities from all four car windows, stuck their naked backsides out of the car's small port holes and then churned up the playing fields with their wheelies and fast revving races. Susanna and the girls could do nothing except keep out of their way and look on in terror and disgust.

One thing she is certain – had they remained standing still, the boys would have run them all down. Another thing that is certain – of course the families of the four boys, blamed Susanna!

The first time Susanna appeared in court, she had to wait with these families. Susanna is much too polite to retell the conversations she had with these people during the time they all had to wait before being admitted into the courtroom.

After the fifth court appearance, the dramas began. The magistrate had seen fit to impose many punishments on the driver, but only issued warnings to his three passengers. Returning home that night the following scenario occurred:

First telephone call: driver of the car abusing Susanna for taking him to court.

Next phone call five minutes later: female pretending to be one of Susanna's students stating that, "We had all lied in court and should change our statements." Susanna had been puzzled by this ploy. Of course, it had not really been one of her students!

Next phone call five minutes later: driver telling Susanna that he had taped her conversations and would be suing her for slander and wrongful conviction.

Next phone call five minutes later: call for the husband from driver telling him his wife was having an affair with a well-known politician at that time. Husband hadn't believed him and had just laughed before re-housing the receiver.

Susanna had then disconnected her phone.

Half an hour later: Susanna hears an horrendous crashing sound as a brick flies through her children's bedroom window, narrowly missing one, had been sleeping, child. Looking out of the window Susanna sees the four boys standing across from the house yelling abuse at her. They throw a second brick into her bedroom window, followed by a flaming paper torch, that struck the curtains causing them to immediately catch alight.

In short, fire trucks, police cars, police officers and a team of detectives could not stop these boys from venting their wrath on this quiet, shy little sport's teacher that night. They kept up their mayhem unrelentingly.

The court case had ended on the Friday night at 3.30pm and the mayhem had started at 4pm. By 2am on the Saturday night, Susanna had been forced to flee her residence with her family. The driver, however, had then pursued her to her new accommodation, phoning her room all weekend, every hour on the hour, yelling abuse at her in his native tongue.

By 7pm on the Sunday night, the police officer in charge of the original case, finally managed to arrest the driver, who was then charged with causing damage and harassment. His case is another saga.

In such situations, it takes a while to emotionally recover from such events. Susanna had felt bad that she couldn't keep her family safe. It was to be a good twelve months before she finally let the memories of that terrifying weekend leave her memory banks.

Saga 18
Expect the Unexpected

Susanna is on a liquid diet today, following her dental appointment. Susanna's regular dentist has inconsiderately taken maternity leave, leaving an unknown male to man her schedules during her absence.

Now, Susanna knows why she preferred her regular dentist.

She's not squirmish! As a child, she used to have fillings without injections! She never had gas for extractions. No, she can handle most dental pain. She told the over – zealous fill-in this, this morning. So, what happened?

Firstly, she arrives in time for her early, early appointment. Secondly, she waits half an hour while the errant locum gets out of bed.

Thirdly, she listens to his recount to the receptionist of an episode that happened the previous day when a patient in his care had, had an allergic reaction to a substance he had used in her mouth. Apparently, it had taken the lady a full hour to respond to the adrenalin treatment given to rectify the allergic reaction – he just couldn't see that it was his fault!

Fourthly, Susanna is summoned to the chair – oh, no, it's him! She hadn't met this locum before and hadn't realised she was this man's first patient of the day. Lucky Susanna!

A simple procedure – a quick fill of a tooth that had broken, causing a small hole in the tooth. On inspection by this young man, very young man, an X-ray or two were taken. *Not sure why*, Susanna thinks.

Tooth filled after a nasty injection given in lip! Again, *Not sure why*, Susanna thinks!

"The tooth has had root canal treatment and is dead," the charming young man had explained to her after giving the totally unnecessary numbing injection.

Susanna leaves, later than expected – mouth very sore and numb. (Paying more than expected! Oh, that's right – all those add-ons!)

"Panadol please… now… urgently!" Susanna almost yells at the pharmacist.

Four hours later, when the injection begins to wear off – why did it take so long? Her regular dentist's ones are fast working!

Susanna is in terrible pain – mouth bleeding – nasty bruising – bad tearing on inner lip – very swollen lip on inside and external. Susanna emails photos of the monstrosity to the dentist – no response – funny that!

Susanna goes out tutoring feeling embarrassed about her facial disfigurement. Arrives home and reflects on her day:

No breakfast
Coffee at 11 – couldn't drink it!
Lunch at 1pm. Couldn't eat it!
Tea at 5 – yum, thanks friend 1!
Wine at 8 – thanks friend 2!
No dinner!

(These two friends had given Susanna gifts of tea and wine – they both know me too well.)

So lucky to have friends. She hopes her face will improve by tomorrow! She hopes her day will too!

Addendum

Susanna reflects on her dental visit last week. Still suffering from the effects of it, as well as being several pounds lighter due to an inability to eat, she wonders if others experience similar situations. If they have, were they expecting them to happen?

Susanna has learnt to expect the unexpected! When faced with a situation one is not expecting, how does one react?

After her recent dental catastrophe, Susanna is now seriously wondering if the young dentist received his training in Australia or overseas – she is favouring the latter! In one conversation she had with the young man, if one can actually call mouth open, cotton padding stuffing lining mouth, tongue at the back of the throat and metal gadgets poking, pricking and prodding – a conversation! He had talked incessantly about dentists who drilled healthy teeth for practice on unsuspecting patients. Unable to actively engage in this conversation, she had remained open-mouthed and non-conversive!

"What? Is he serious? Where was this?" she was left contemplating? "Not in Australia she hoped!"

Susanna also wonders what her usual, lovely dentist will say, think, do, when she learns of Susanna's episode. Susanna smiles, "She owns the business, so she **will** find out!"

So, let's move on to other situations one is not expecting. Are visits to the doctor as traumatic as Susanna's recent dental one, or does she sail through these with ease?

Women undergo regular highly invasive procedures under the guise of preventative measures! Do we really need such careful monitoring of our most private and sensitive anatomical features? Well, who knows? We are certainly castigated by the medical professionals, if we don't comply. Susanna has understood, of late, that so much of the modern monitoring methodologies now are just really 'jobs for the boys'! She can recall many circumstances in which she has declined to proceed further with investigatory procedures because – the referral was to a 'mate' of the referring doctor – hey, is this ethical?

Another ploy is for bulk-billing medical centres to entice patients to attend for regular monitoring of moles, cysts or benign lumps, knowing that kind Mr Medicare will pay them handsomely at no outlay from the patient. Susanna once attended at one cancer clinic for four consecutive months until she finally twigged it was a scam! (Hey, some people like the attention – hey again, some people feel they are important – even wearing their best clothes, when they attend for medical appointments.) Susanna – no, she has no delusions and dislikes the attention.

Perhaps that's why she gets it! No, not 'gets it' – **gets it** – attention, that is!
It's always her, and it will, **always** be her!

Incident 1

Susanna was required to attend for a medical examination in Sydney. Three other teachers at the school, where she worked, also had to attend at the same venue and time. The four colleagues travelled into the city together. They chatted happily on the train, enjoyed a coffee in the adjacent cafe to the medical centre and sat patiently until they were called. All called within two minutes of waiting – all allocated individual doctors, the three colleagues all reseating themselves in the waiting room two minutes later. So, what happened to Susanna?

Why was it that she was allocated the 70-year-old, retired male medic? Was it just the luck of the draw?

An hour later Susanna surfaces from his consulting rooms to face the annoyance of her patiently – perhaps now not so patient – fellow teachers. Journeying back to their school, Susanna had asked them all about their medical examinations.

"Oh, we just had to sign some papers!" was all each of them said.

If Susanna hadn't, had to get back to school that day for her classes, she would have made a complaint.

So, what had happened?

On walking in, she had been ordered to undress behind a screen. The doctor had deliberately brushed past the screen, opening the curtain just a fraction, just enough to allow himself to watch surreptitiously – Susanna had caught his eye as she had removed her underwear. Naked, she had presented for a physical workout program first. This had involved touching her toes facing the doctor as well as with her back to him. This latter procedure involved him running his fingers from north to south of her body and through all the bits in between! (Hey, there's a name for this now!)

Susanna was then asked to lie on her back on the examination table. She is not going to describe what happened here – not appropriate – the name for the above activity (activity?) is the same.

The doctor knew he could get away with it! Susanna had left feeling horribly violated and physically ill.

In her life, though, Susanna has experienced extremely bad sexual encounters, and so gets over these unexpected incidents quickly.

Incident 2

Fairly recently Susanna was attending a medical centre which included a team of close to retirement male doctors. Susanna's choice had been a lovely gentleman of Anglo-Saxon background who had chosen to only work on Fridays. So, her appointment was for a Friday – early. So early – no one else was there at that time!

The appointment was for a full medical examination plus the usual, obligatory monitoring of female features. Of course, Susanna hadn't requested these services – rather she had been summoned to the surgery.

Once again, she found herself naked – he hadn't required this on previous occasions! Hmm! OK – the top half examination seems to be more thorough than usual! Hmm! The lower section examination – "OK, so why do I have to remain unclothed while I'm now standing next to him as he bends down to open a drawer adjacent to my knees?"

"Oh, **he** wasn't expecting **that**!"

Understanding the doctor's reaction to her naked physical presence, Susanna had quickly dressed and left. She hasn't returned since to that surgery!

So, Susanna, which is the lesser of the two evils?

Without a shadow of a doubt, Pelly, the **dentist!**

Saga 19
The Renta Nanny

> It is school holidays for Susanna at the moment. On the one hand she enjoys the opportunity to stay home for longer and not have to endure the lengthy drives to and from work each day, yet on the other hand she always finds herself looking after other people's children in some capacity. She doesn't mind this – *she likes children – she chose to be a teacher – so stop complaining! she thinks.*
> Much of her weekend time, when she's not working, is looking after her granddaughter, which, of course she loves doing, but the weekend just past moved into the era of summer Daylight Saving. This meant that Susanna became the babysitter for much longer and would continue to until the clocks returned to sun time.

As Susanna reflects on her weekend, she can honestly say it was one of the longest on record, made longer by the now unchallenged institution called Daylight Saving.

When Susanna first arrived in Australia, she was called upon by the government to vote in a referendum. Not being fully aware of the benefits, or the disadvantages, she conducted her own research to find out what her new 'Aussie' counterparts preferred.

Without a second's hesitation, the majority of every man and his dog in New South Wales voted to retain this 'so-called benefit'.

But is it a benefit? Susanna had pondered this. In the United Kingdom (where Susanna grew up) the clocks were changed for safety reasons – they were adjusted by an hour in October, to enable children to walk home from school before it got too dark. She believes this is still so today. Yes, that makes sense!

So, why do Aussies fanatically support this time alteration – the beach, of course! What else? (So, why doesn't the tropical state support this? – a rhetorical question Susanna knows the answer to but asks it suggestively anyway!)

Well, do NSW country folk think the same? Their argument held little weight with the pollies – "I wonder why?" Susanna smiles. "Perhaps it's because they thought there was some divine intervention! No, seriously folks, many country residents wrote letters complaining their curtains faded more during daylight saving hours!"

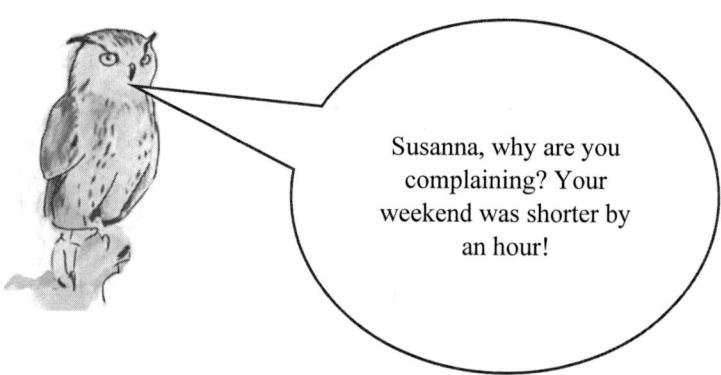

Susanna, why are you complaining? Your weekend was shorter by an hour!

"I know," she grimaces, "But each day now just keeps going on… and on…! I have breakfast later, coffee time creeps up immediately when I'm not expecting it, afternoon tea gets pushed aside and dinner bosses in unwanted!"

What does all this have to do with your saga? Quit complaining and start writing!

OK!

So, what is a renta nanny?

Susanna discovered this interesting facet a while ago when she was invited to attend her grandson's special Grandparents' Day at his school. At the time, he was attending day-care, a program he absolutely loved. Being just three years old, Xavi had excitedly asked his nanny to come and see him at school.

"Nanny, you'll love it. We will have hayrides and pumpkin patch!" His eyes had implored hers.

"Great!" Susanna had looked dolefully at this hopeful child, but had secretly thought, *I get hay fever!*

Xavi, noticing his nanny's slight hesitation, continued his plea. "Nanny, everyone's grandparents will be there!" He had then hugged his grandma.

So, what could she do? Of course, she had to go!

And so it was that the next day she set off. Following implicit instructions from her daughter, as to how to locate the venue for the event, Susanna arrived at her grandson's classroom. She spied Xavi immediately, who was smiling broadly at her, and selected one of the vacant seats positioned within the room to wait patiently for the other guests to arrive.

The teacher too waited patiently, smiling nervously at Susanna.

"Well, where were they all?" Susanna asked herself, as she scanned the length and breadth of the room. "Anywhere, apparently, but here!" she wryly curled her lip, allowing a slight smirk to creep across her face.

"We'll just wait and see if anyone else turns up," the teacher then nodded in the direction of Susanna, who knew full well what the young lady was thinking – of all her grandparents who could have been present today, the one person she hadn't wanted present **was** well and truly present! Susanna being a very practised specialist teacher has never had any problems managing groups of children, unlike this lady who – not being a trained teacher – had great difficulty coping with the behavioural episodes her young charges were presenting her with. (Well, they were excited!)

Xavi, of course, had explained in great detail to his teacher, all about his nanny. She was aware Susanna had been a school principal, so understandably the lady felt a little under pressure to perform well.

"Let's get this show on the road!" Susanna finally announces to the eagerly eying ankle-biters, when it is blatantly obvious nothing else is going to happen. She admits, though, that three-year-old rompers are not really her preferred age of children – being a high school teacher initially, she has a much better rapport with older students, but today this is what she has to work with!

And so it was that the 'renta nanny' arrived – this wonderful person who instantly grabs the attention of the children, sings them songs, reads them stories, plays jumping games, colours in their pictures with them, holds their hands as they show her their projects and then accommodates them sitting on her lap (all 30 of them) while they bump along in the hay cart.

On exiting the cart, the excited group of littlies had then raced their renta nanny to the pumpkin patch to find her the biggest pumpkin, which was instantly presented to her with oodles of cuddles, kisses and hugs. The renta nanny had been allowed to depart at this stage, receiving a well-deserved thank you and smile from the now, not so nervous, young teacher. With the nanny shift over, Susanna had then driven home to rest!

"But it's never over!" Susanna once again grimaces, as she sits in the children's play area of her granddaughter's preschool waiting quietly for all the other grandparents to arrive. This child, a two-year-old, nearly the same age that her grandson was when Susanna graced her presence at his preschool, sat keenly watching her nanny.

A few parents sauntered in, followed by a handful of elderly folk – presumably grandparents, but as none of them made any move to interact with any child in the room, it was difficult to ascertain the reason they were there.

Once again, the renta nanny is called upon to be the morning's entertainment, as she sings their songs, lets them show her around their play areas, makes sandcastle cakes, draws them all funny sketches, shares their snacks, gives them all donkey rides and finally leaves exhausted. *I'm getting too old for this!* Susanna thinks, as she drives out of the car park. *Home for a shower and coffee!*

"Because every day, Pelly, was renta nanny day!"

Saturday, Susanna found herself looking after children in her house from early morning until early afternoon, when it was time to venture down to the park. "The park is great, Pelly, but why do the grandparents just expect to be allowed to just sit and sip their coffees – Susanna is never permitted this indulgence! What does she do wrong?"

Susanna had watched with interest the swarms of elderly folk, who had carefully carried their steaming cups of cappuccinos, located nice, comfortable seats with which to seat themselves at safe distances from their adorable grandchildren, and prepared themselves for a lengthy session of smiling, nodding and slurping, as their young charges played.

"So, why don't **they** play with their grandchildren Pelly?"

"Yes, Zebbie, but why the same the next day?"

Sunday, Susanna had agreed to accompany her son, his wife and their little girl to the local swimming centre. The pools are heated, which is great for the little paddlers.

Susanna's granddaughter loves to paddle around in the baby pool. She especially loves it when her nanny joins in too. But, how come, within seconds of entering the water – the pair are suddenly inundated with splashers, jumpers and throwers of all shapes and sizes – all keen to join them? Were their games not as exciting as the ones Susanna and her charge were playing? Obviously not!

Susanna, what happened on Monday?

Monday, Cuthbert, Susanna was supposed to have had a special day out with friends, but this was postponed. She didn't want to waste her tickets, so she gave them to her son to use.

Susanna's son had been excited at the opportunity to take his daughter and her mum out for the day. The tickets were for the Science Space Centre. He had never been and was interested to see what exhibits, shows and programs were on offer. They arrived at the centre early and booked in their shows. It was at the point when his little two-year-old was seated in the planetarium, ready for the show to start, that she had suddenly realised her poor nanny was sitting at home alone and missing out on all the fun! (Oh, dear, what a pity – never mind. Susanna would have been quite happy doing that!)

But, no – poor nanny – she must be summoned immediately!

And so, it was that the renta nanny obediently presented for duty. And, of course, it didn't take long before the hordes gathered for their day of fun with her too. Within seconds of arriving at the Science Space Centre, Susanna had found herself surrounded by dozens of littlies – pushers, shovers, kickers, leaners, sitters, pokers, prodders, snifflers and snugglers – all eager, apparently, to have the renta nanny's attention, while their parents and grandparents, presumably, indulged themselves in the cafés, or watched one of the shows – she never knew which or what, who they were, or what they did, because she never saw any of them!

The happy children all built tall skyscrapers, designed vehicles of every description and dimension, and played weird space odyssey games.

> Oh, come on, Susanna! Tell me you had fun!

"Yes, Bear. Susanna does her best. The children's parents, though, had booked tickets for them to see shows! So, why hadn't they seen the shows?"

Her granddaughter had decided that playing with her nanny would be more interesting than watching the giant fly in the planetarium show – Susanna gets that! But… she **was** a tad curious where the parents were of the children who had congregated around her and her granddaughter – the children had literally – appeared from nowhere like a swarm of bees around a honey pot.

When Susanna had returned home that night, it had been quite late. With Daylight Saving now in place, parents naturally want to stay out later, the sun is still warm in the late afternoon and so the day becomes – longer. Parents don't want to go home, if their kids are being – well entertained! (Susanna gets that!)

Reflecting on her long weekend – yes, it had been a 'long' weekend!

The renta nanny had done her shifts and she had done her best!

No wonder she's thinking of working in the UK next year!

Saga 20
The Perfect Day!

> With daylight saving fully entrenched, Susanna can at least attempt to enjoy the extended hours of daylight. It is an opportunity to get out and about, be a little more social and look forward to her well-earned holiday break – she has saved up a little money for this. This saga reflects on 'the perfect day'!

So, what makes the perfect day? Susanna often wonders where her next saga will take her. Will it tell of her wonderful exploits into realms unknown; will it excite her growing list of readers who avidly read her tales of woe so faithfully – always smiling politely at her when they say they have read the latest rendition; will it reflect her busy social life – filled with juicy gossipy items most people relish and devour so greedily, or will it just be a whinge? Well, sorry folks, it's not any of these!

Sagas are opportunities to share! The world is an unsafe place and one in which we all need to protect ourselves from those intent on doing us harm! Susanna's sagas allow her the opportunity to whine away her whinges, something today she has ample of.

She always knows what kind of day she will have by the hour at which she re-joins the living world. On a good day, the ideal time is around 3am. This means she has slept wonderfully for an amazing five hours – oh, such bliss! At this hour, she can play Scrabble, read the latest snippets about the fantastic lives her friends seem to be leading on Face Book (so fantastic, apparently, that they feel the need to share every picture of a toilet they visited, mouthful of food they consumed or child they felt the need to share their selfie with) browse the Google goss spots or simply lie there and listen to her songs for an hour before it's coffee time!

Susanna loves that first morning brew. She likes it not too strong, not too weak, not too sweet but extremely hot and decaf and without milk. Yum! Yum, yummy! The smooth as silk liquid simply glides down, revitalising her senses and generating endorphins. This special, alone time is precious and treasured before she knows the onslaught of the day will soon arrive.

This perfect time prepares her perfectly placed to greet the new day in a positive light, chat briefly to her pretty flowers, communicate with her on-line friends and enjoy a delicious bowl of fresh fruit and cereal. Wow! How lucky is she?

Well, was she lucky today? What time did she wake up? What went wrong?

1. She woke up at 1.30am – bugger – bugger off daylight saving!
2. The on-line computer slaughtered her at Scrabble.
3. What are these 'stupid' words he makes anyway?
4. Her headphones went on strike.
5. They said it was too early for music!
6. The neighbour isn't talking to her – no emails! Bad sign – means she's upset that Susanna fed her cat the night before.
7. The dog across the way won't stop barking! Shut up yer mongrel!
8. It's too early for coffee!

So, all things considered, it's going to be the perfect day!
Fell asleep.
Overslept – never oversleep!
Bad headache.
Missed breakfast.

Roads very busy – where have all these people come from? Traffic bad on M1 today. Must be coming back from their southerly sojourns.

Accident on the intersection leading to work premises – running late for lesson.

No petrol – is that what that little petrol pump means. – Never knew that! No petrol station near. Great.

But… Yes, the perfect lesson. The perfect student. The perfect house. The perfect location. Thank you, Chloe – you made my day!

Arriving home, though, back to this planet.

Susanna asks herself why she is drinking wine at 3.45pm. The rules are 5pm. "Well, I'm breaking them today!" she defiantly snorts. "Sometimes it's allowed!"

The perfect little day continues.

Phone call from some IT company telling Susanna her subscription is due. Bad mistake to answer these types of calls! But…how does one know?

In 2016 a company formed in the US but based in Barcelona, crashed Susanna's computer. To fix it, they told her it would cost $600 USD. At the time she had no choice but to pay – her computer was virused.

The scam is this:

They infect your computer.

They fix it for a fair amount.

They do nothing for 2 years.

They then phone and say your subscription needs renewing.

They tell you that you have a five-year plan.

The total cost is 4000 USD if you cancel. If you don't, it is 8000 USD.

Susanna refuted the agreement, but the company used her card anyway to direct debit her account. Ouch!

Friends:

Never buy on-line

Never give any personal information through internet outlets

Protect your on-line information with undetectable passwords.

Susanna now has no computer and is considerably poorer. Having spent all afternoon talking to fraud and scam police, she is left with only the lesson to learn! Hence the wine, which by the way, is delicious! She saved a very special bottle for just this perfect little moment.

Susanna reflects. It's no good complaining. It's no good feeling annoyed or sorry. What's done is done! So, sorry friends, you get the benefit of my 'perfect little day'. No sooner had Susanna put the phone down from the scammers – they phoned a zillion times and emailed a multitude of times, a pension notice arrived in the post advising of a fall in interest rates resulting in a loss of income this quarter, and her computer crashed as a result of the scammers being annoyed with Susanna's attitude.

"Bugger – now have to fix the computer!" Susanna yells out loudly.

So, how does the perfect little day end.

No computer for a week

No debit card to access any cash

A fee to have technicians fix her computer

No holiday now, as money gone to scammers

But… At the end of the day… Susanna has the perfect drop of her favourite sparkly, which makes everything – perfect!

Thus ends – 'The Perfect Day'!

An Addendum

Susanna was able to re-claim a large portion of these scammed funds – much happier now!

Saga 21
Road Rage

> Susanna's students frequently comment to her that she leads a very exciting life, when they discover all the stories she tells them are true. Yes, believe it or not!

Whilst driving to a winery a few hours' drive south from her home at the weekend, Susanna witnessed a horrible road accident involving a truck and a motor cyclist. In Susanna's brief glimpse, it seemed to her that the truck was annoyed the motorcyclist had dared to overtake him, and so had gone 'on the chase'!

Sadly, it had been the motorcyclist that had lost, not just this fight, but also his life!

Why is it that trucks feel they have 'the power?' Does size matter? Yes of course it does. Susanna is reminded of an earlier incident last week, whilst driving to work. She is still seeking answers from Roads and Maritime Services to ascertain how she 'apparently' was at fault.

It was early afternoon. At this time of day, mothers are preparing to pick up children from school, truckies are filling up their tanks and their stomachs and Susanna is heading north. Approaching a petrol station, adjacent to camera traffic lights at a speed of 53 Km, Susanna is 10 metres behind the car immediately in front of hers. This car is slowing to stop at the lights, when a truck suddenly decides to pull out from the petrol station to sneak in between this car and Susanna's.

Susanna too was slowing to prepare to stop at the lights, but she wasn't prepared for the expectation of the truck driver for her to make accommodations for his sizeable commercial road train, that had she had the capacity to do so, would still have taken up all three laneways, inconveniencing more than just her vehicle, if Susanna had permitted him to continue pulling out at that precise moment.

It wasn't that Susanna deliberately meant to provoke the truck driver. She simply didn't have the time and distance to give him access. Her question is, "Should she have automatically given him this right of way?" She asked herself this, as she stopped behind the car immediately in front of her, now stationary at the traffic lights.

She would have thought nothing more of the incident, except her own curiosity for the truck driver's overtly rude hand signals and verbally vile language directed at Susanna, not just at this initial location, but afterwards for some kilometres heading north, before he finally turned off, heading west. The man had obviously been expecting Susanna to immediately give him priority access.

So, was Susanna in the wrong?

For Susanna to have pulled up sharply, at his point of entering the highway, would have caused the car behind Susanna to have smashed into her rear! She is absolutely, certain of that. This car was very close and matching her speed.

After scanning the rules for trucks on the internet, Susanna was unable to locate any information pertaining to priority access for trucks exiting petrol stations when wishing to re-join highway traffic.

The behaviour of the truckie, at the exact time Susanna's vehicle passed his truck, and for the next few minutes following, once he had successfully positioned his monstrous vehicle into the traffic, could only be considered bullying and harassment, as well as noise pollution – thumping his horn aggressively at her!

However, undeterred, Susanna still feels she did the 'right' thing. To have stopped sharply, as he had expected her to do, would have caused an accident. "Sorry, mate!"

But why should he have cared if that had been the outcome? He wouldn't have! He would have casually cruised out, leaving the mess behind him, and laughing at his own sense of power.

Well, the outcome was that Susanna apparently retained the 'sense of power' which he had tried to get back from her through his Road Rage Rants.

Yeah, move on!

Susanna is reminded, though, that it seems to be the 'Aussie' way to get away with what you can. This is not said or meant maliciously but simply as an observation.

A particularly annoying example of this attitude currently exists in the complex where Susanna lives. The Strata Management By-Laws specifically deny residents access to the visitor parking bays, as each unit has a double garage, suitable for accommodating two small – medium-sized vehicles.

These laws advise residents that the fine for the first infringement is $1000, which doubles every day following.

"So, how come one resident is permitted to park exclusively in one visitor bay for three months?" Susanna enquired of Strata Management one day. This lady had developed the habit of parking in one bay whilst her work mate picked her up, the two ladies travelling to work together leaving the incoming car in the same spot. This lady had deliberately orchestrated for herself to acquire an exclusive parking space additional to her allocation.

Strata Management had then advised residents that they could actually lease one of these spaces for a fee of $10,000 per year. Needless to say, this lady declined this offer, moved her car and then her house! At no time did she care that she had done the 'wrong' thing – she was only annoyed that she had been caught!

But, of course, Susanna knows only too well, that when one problem is solved, another one appears immediately. Once the errant lady had moved out, another resident decided to park both his cars in the only available visitor bays – for visitors!

So, once again Susanna makes herself somewhat unpopular by seeking Strata Management action to force this man to do the 'right' thing.

The question that begs itself on all these and similar circumstances is though, 'Why is it that those who do the wrong thing, blame the whistle blower, when they are caught?'

Susanna knows the answer to this question: because it's the Aussie way!

Again, this statement is not said maliciously or unkindly – simply amusedly.

Another situation in her residential complex pertains to her immediate neighbour, who has set up a dog clipping salon in her garage on one side, and a hairdressing salon on the other side. To do this she knocked down walls using government money given to her as pension money. To make internal structural alterations requires approval from Strata Management, which was not sought. To use her garage for alternative purposes other than storage of cars and detritus is against council regulations – but hey, who cares?

Susanna smiles, "The residents might if they knew their insurance premiums would rise steeply, if they had to accommodate the indemnity insurances for both of this resident's businesses!"

Oh, well, that's a fight for another day!

Saga 22
A Rude Interruption to Her Working Life

To the world, working is a rude interruption to one's social life. To children, homework is a rude interruption to their social and play times. So, why does Susanna not see it this way, when everyone else clearly does? It's not that she's anti-social, she just does not have time for it!

To the working world, Monday is the nadir! The servants reluctantly trudge wearily and unenthusiastically off to the salt mines to begin another week of whatever it is they do, that they call 'work'! Susanna would always be amused when she listened to conversations in which the conversant would utter, "I've worked so hard today, I've earned my wine," when Susanna had known only too well the lady conversant had idled her time chatting socially for most of it.

And ... as the working week progresses, spirits are lifted – not just spiritually, but 'spiritually' as the eager, beaver pay checkers scramble quickly to the many cafés and bars to reward themselves for their day's and week's efforts. Oh, how they long for those Friday night drinks at the pub, followed by the weekend 'barbie' and then the obligatory Sunday brunch before retiring to rest with rellies watching their favourite footie team. And ... of course the obligatory celebratory beer or two doesn't go amiss at these times!

To Susanna, she always cringes when people ask her what her weekend plans are. *Weekend plans! Are they mad*! she thinks? In today's society, though, it does seem to loom high on everyone's agenda that weekend plans are an absolute must. Without something exciting to retort, or report, each week, do people feel they have failed socially? Do they feel they must organise at least one party, just to keep up their social status?

Well, Susanna does not think this way – she is a working zealot, which is why last weekend was not an event she wanted, looked forward to or dared to brag about. So, what did she do?

She went to lunch!

Recently, she was invited to attend a birthday lunch – hers! Yes, birthdays have a lot to answer for – those social times that one finds too difficult to avoid. The drive was two and a half hours on the outward journey and two hours home, making the day almost entirely social. When Susanna had indicated to her hosts that she would not be able to leave until 11am, due to work commitments, they were somewhat peeved – well that's not actually the word that comes to mind immediately that describes their reactions, but it's a word with the same beginning and ending letters!

So, why were these people confused as to why their friend, and family member, required this work time?

Susanna knows it's because people who are not teachers, have no understanding of what is required when a lesson needs to be taught. For the specialist nature of Susanna's schedules, it can take in excess of two hours to prepare highly detailed task analyses of skills to be taught successfully, together with accompanying practical tasks, for one child alone, let alone the agenda of other students she shares learning time with. There are parents who believe a lesson begins when a child sits down with the teacher – no – wrong! The lesson begins when Susanna sits down to write it!

Is this paid time? No.

So, why does she do it?

Do all teachers spend this much time on one lesson? No. Susanna does, mostly because many of her students struggle with their learning and do need a task analysis approach. The majority of teachers prepare their lessons beforehand, but do not attribute too much time to this unpaid overtime.

She repeats… why does she do it?

Because it **is** what she does! It **is** why she has come to this planet at this time in the evolution of her life! It **is** her joy and absolute passion. She still remembers the feeling of pride when she donned the blue sash denoting education, at her graduation ceremony. Blue is her favourite colour depicted in all things she holds dear that are of educational value to her. She has enormous respect and pride for what she does 'educationally' for her students. She strives to be 'the best'! You can't be the best if you don't actively train for it with every ounce of energy and commitment you can give! To give up a Sunday to social, takes away such precious training time – people just don't get that! They get it if one is training for the Olympics. To Susanna, it's the same thing. (She won't rant on about this – she knows you get it!)

So, Susanna has struggled this week. With no time to prepare lesson curricula, she is left only to splatter her matters on paper and subject her 'friends' to her social rants – sorry.

So, Susanna, what are your weekend plans? Hee, hee!

Well, bear, as you've asked, I am assisting a student and her team to prepare for a highly auspicious Science and Technology initiative.

Addendum: Her team won! There were teams from across the world competing.

Saga 23
The Big Day Out

This story is dedicated to the Irwins. I promised them I'd write a saga about one of our days out.

Susanna could have chosen this, but she felt her friends may have found this a little 'too' exhilarating!

She was going to choose this, but decided the water was a little 'too' cool for her at this time of year.

No, she thought she had better play safe and choose something 'educational' instead.

How boring! Make sure you're inside – it's freezing outside!

Yes, Lenny, we will be fine.

No! Susanna never takes that stupid thing. On the one occasion she did, she ended up sky-high, literally 'blown away'! – another saga!

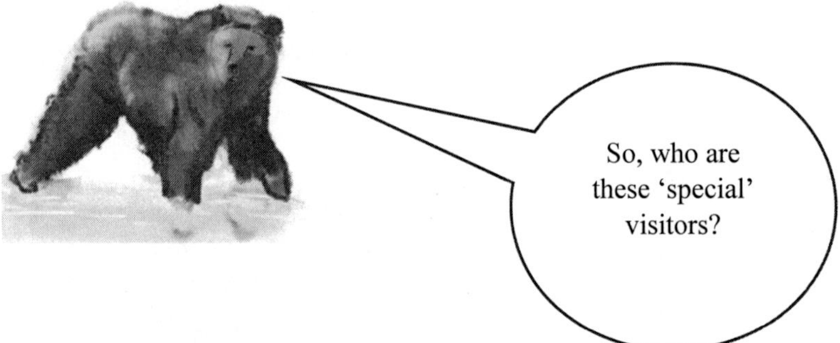

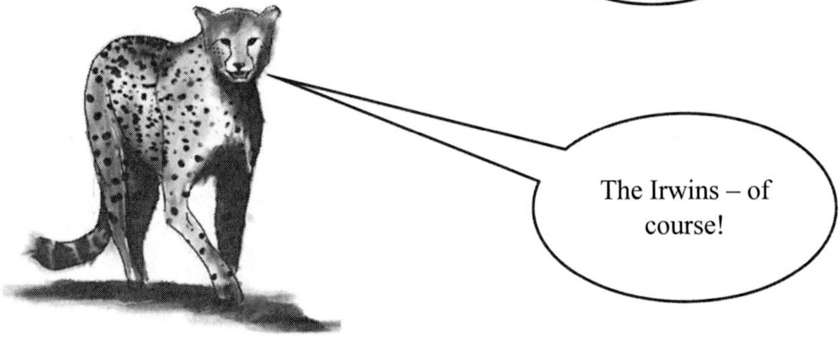

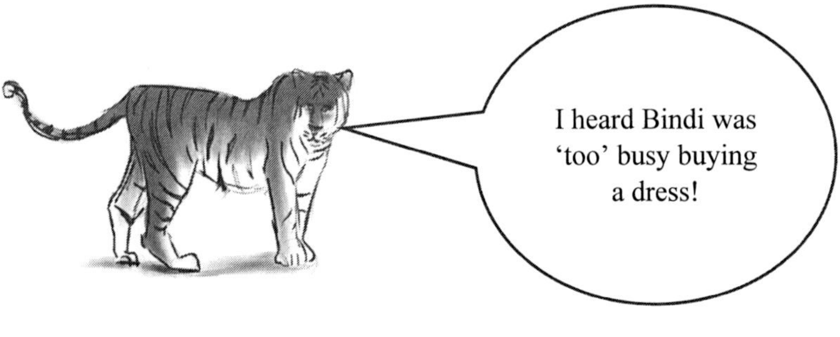

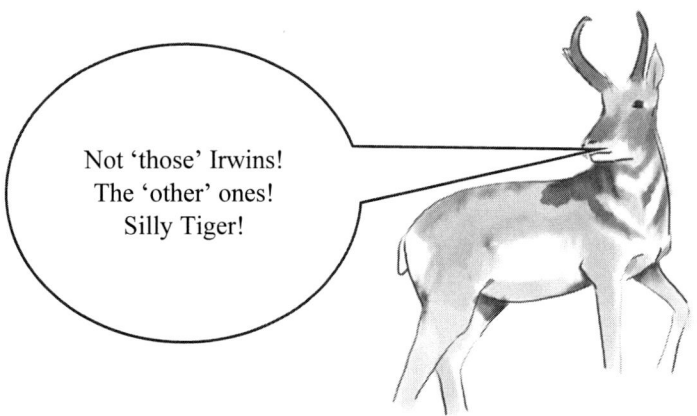

And so, Susanna's day out started.

"Oh, goody," she reads the text message – "they're late. That means I can have breakfast!"

The entourage arrives in style. New car! Susanna notices. Nice! Same as hers – but better!

They head off quickly, not to be late for the bubbles and balloons show at the Science Centre in Wollongong.

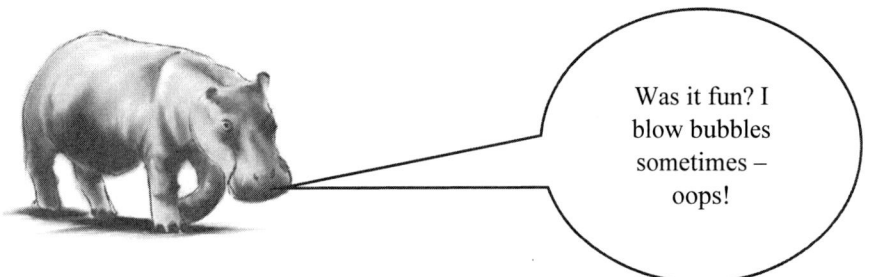

Yes, animals, the bubbles and balloons were fun!

The group then quickly assembled in the planetarium for the start of the show 'Perfect Little Planet'.

Susanna wonders how people can actually watch these 3D/4D reality video presentations. Not only was the speed of the characters and machines through space so fast, but the commentary was also fast paced. This was one poor, aging lady who could not cope! The younger set seemed to have no trouble. The thing that Susanna was left with, apart from a gigantic migraine headache, was thinking it quite odd that in all our universe, we seem to be the only planet with such an amazing assortment of resources and creations – simply incomprehensible! Seriously, how lucky are we?

So, on to the next show.

Oh, no – they all want drinks!

"No, Susanna, we all want food!"

"Didn't you eat breakfast?" she asks?

"Yes."

"So, what meal is this?" the extremely regimented and disciplined lady quietly keeps her thoughts to herself.

She enjoys a nice coffee, all the same. Why not!

"It's freezing here!" she grimaces as she sits in the outdoor space within the Science Centre. *How the days change from one to the next. She's glad she has a jacket in the car,* she thinks as she smiles at her group of happy campers eagerly wolfing down their little snacks.

Show two: 'We are all Stars.'

This would have been wonderful, if Susanna could have opened her eyes at least for more than two seconds. These amazing graphic presentations are so interesting to listen to, which was all she could do, that she is left pondering why there is so much controversy surrounding how the stars and the planets were created. The scientific explanation is so logical and plausible. Great – loved it – just couldn't watch it!

So, what next? The Science Centre has two floors of exhibits for children to try their luck, skill or just browse. By this time the floors were both becoming busy and noisy. The group decides to move to the quieter Biology theatre to taste a few caterpillars, make a grotesque bug or grow a botanical garden. Here the aging lady sits and watches the kids create their wonderful masterpieces, and to proudly show them off to their mum and her afterwards. Yes, time well spent.

Those caterpillars sound juicy!

Lunch time!

"Lunch, we don't want lunch!" the kids scream.

"But it's what we've come to do!" Susanna looks agog! "It's what our day out is all about! We're going to the pub!"

Oh, no! the girls look dismayed and openly aggrieved, so aggrieved that one of them leaves her bag in the Centre accidentally.

The luncheoners head south. Shellharbour is a pretty tourist village. Susanna had lived there briefly and had enjoyed this treasured time with her husband. On a warm, sunny day it is perfect to sit and watch the waves from the restaurant, which is what they did, except it wasn't a perfect day, weather wise.

"Once again," Susanna grimaces. "Why can't restaurants get it right? It's not hard to take a booking. And... hello! Why is this young girl blaming me for their staff not taking the booking correctly? And... hello again! She's now telling us this is her first day! I wonder how long she'll last?" Susanna verbalises her thoughts as she and her guests are finally seated somewhere, she didn't book – her choice of seating had been an inobtrusive window seating table for four. Instead they were plonked down somewhere obtrusive.

"Not good enough Ocean Beach Hotel!" Susanna snarls privately to herself.

"Oh, well, the food had better be good!" Susanna quietly watches the waiters and patiently sips her delicious icy-cold treat bought for her by her guests... and, yes it was! They got that right! Thank you, Margaret, lovely lunch!

All good. Great, actually. The group eats a hearty lunch, telephones the Centre to ask them to locate the errant bag, and then heads back to collect it.

"We might as well stay here, Susanna," the group smiles at her as they retrieve the bag. "We're here now and we have an hour to browse. Can we please...pretty please?"

"Yes, why not!" Susanna looks at their eager beaver faces. "It's all they really want to do."

And so, it was that the last hour of the day was spent poking, prodding, pushing, shoving, jumping, peering, sliding, squeezing every possible knob in both sections of the two floors. Susanna's favourite exhibit was the kids' wall building activity. Here the littlies could don hard hats, pulley up their bricks, or lift them onto the conveyor belt to the top level, sort them into their different colours and designs and build a monstrous wall. It required the children to work together to perform various job roles – children who not knowing each other at the start, instantly became close work buddies, building creative constructions of varying sizes, shapes and colours. Susanna loved seeing them take each task seriously, especially using the pulley and wheelbarrow to feed fodder to the builders.

Great activity – she can't wait until her granddaughter is old enough to have a go!

But… the witching hour approaches. Time to leave and head back to Susanna's.

You told me you were going to the park!

"I know Polar, but it was freezing!"

Susanna's house has coffee and some games the girls can play.

All good – all went well – all had fun – she hoped – all went home!

And thus ends 'The Big Day Out'!

Thank you Irwins.

Saga 24
The Fine Print

How often do we get caught? How fine is the fine print? Is it deliberately disguised to trick us?

Recently Susanna has had cause to question the ethics of companies who deliberately use enticing oral advertising campaigns to lure unsuspecting customers into purchasing items they didn't plan to buy, but the offer seemed too good to be true, but after purchasing the package they get caught by 'the fine print'!

Companies are clever at making potential customers feel immensely important prior to a sale, but afterwards treat them with far less respect, if the customer shows dissatisfaction with the product. Companies never want to return money, despite saying they have 'great returns policies'.

Of course, they don't! That would be 'bad business' or 'no business'!

Susanna is well known at the Department of Fair Trading. They will assist consumers to understand what their legal rights are in relation to goods and services purchased in Australia. However, if the consumer chooses to buy products on-line from other countries, no such accommodations or assistance are afforded them. People should generally be cautious about buying items from overseas countries because they know the cost of returning unwanted items can be more than the initial cost of the item.

Susanna was recently caught by an on-line book company based in the UK. Their website displayed several photographs of a book Susanna wished to purchase. There were actually three books that she wished to buy from this on-line store, carefully selecting the preferred cover and costs before checking out.

Two of the books immediately shipped at the advertised shipping cost of the three books. Susanna questioned the company why the third book was not included. Their email information service had quickly responded that the book had to be ordered separately but would be sent within four weeks.

Susanna was happy with the two books that arrived – no problem. No reason to return. Satisfied customer.

Was she happy with the third book? No! Why not? Because it wasn't a book, it was a CD of the book!

On receiving the item, Susanna had immediately checked her order, invoice and email correspondence with the company. Nowhere did the documentation indicate that the product was in audio form.

Yes, the company has a returns policy. Yes the company would provide her with a refund of $12 and yes Susanna must pay the shipping costs of the book back to the UK, and yes they would gladly send her the correct book this time – please accept our apologies – but, yes you will have to pay the shipping costs for your new order.

"Hello, you made the error – you deliberately split my order to deliberately charge me two shipping costs, one for the two books and one for the audio book, and then expect me to pay for the return shipping for the item I clearly did not order, to then pay more shipping for the correct order?" Susanna had politely asked the person she had spoken to on the phone.

"Well madam, the fine print does explain our returns policy to you, and we are just following it!"

"Yes, but you made the error – not me!" Susanna had vehemently exclaimed to the voice at the end of the phone.

The cost of the book was $12. There should have been no additional shipping charges, as Susanna had paid for this with the initial order of three books. The additional shipping rate charged for the audio book was eleven dollars. To return the audio book to receive her $12 refund, the total cost of packaging and postal costs would be $24. "Why would I do this?" she asked herself when she arrived at the post office. "I would get more satisfaction from donating it to a charity shop."

Which she did.

So, reading the fine print – what fine print? Oh, the picture on the website that showed the cover of the book, with the finest of detail in the bottom right-hand corner that said 'audio'.

Susanna had then ordered the book from an Australian company based in Sydney. Why didn't she just do this in the first place? Because she didn't read the fine print regarding location of the company!

As Susanna has stated, she is 'best friends' with several staff members at Fair Trading NSW, who have helped her fully understand the changes to Australian Consumer Law. Under ACL since 2012, all companies guarantee their products and services.

Companies may not like this clause. However, it is law and they must accept it. If a consumer purchases an item in Australia and the item is faulty, the company must accept responsibility. If returning the item to the company falls under the category of 'Major Fault' the purchaser can decide to receive a repair or a refund.

Knowing one's rights under ACL is a very powerful response tool when dealing with conniving salespeople, as Susanna has discovered on more than one occasion. She enjoyed her conversation with one gentleman one day, who was urging her to buy extended warranty on a vacuum cleaner. "Why would I do that," she had smiled at him, "when you guarantee your product!"

"Oh, it doesn't mean that," the nice man had whimpered at his customer. "You need extended warranty because we only guarantee this product for twelve months, after which time you must pay for all repairs."

Susanna had then graciously declined to pay the additional costs of extended warranty, leaving the gentleman with these closing remarks, "Sir, you would do well to read the fine print – your company holds the record for the most fines, and the highest penalty rates, issued through the Australian courts for breaches to ACL! Did you know that?"

He had been glad Susanna had left the shop before other customers overheard her closing remarks to him.

On recalling other situations, the most interesting one Susanna was involved in was 'The Second-Hand Car Episode'.

Susanna had gone shopping for a cheap auto for her husband to get around in. He hadn't driven for many years but had decided a local runabout would be useful. As she was perusing several possible options within a large car yard, a very enthusiastic salesman had approached her.

"Susanna, I have just the car for you. It has just come in, has been thoroughly checked by our workshop and is ready to roll."

"Great, I'll take it."

She had, of course, taken it for a test drive, and it did meet all requirements.

Driving home, however, a warning light had appeared on the dashboard. Checking the handbook, Susanna discovered that this was cause for concern, and so she immediately booked the car into a specialist service for her car make and model. Picking the car up the next day, she had been assured the problem was fixed, and so drove home.

When switching the engine on the next day, she had been alarmed to see the same alarm bell. "Oh, no, not again," she had grimaced, and immediately phoned Fair Trading for advice.

Fair Trading were excellent. They told her exactly what to do, and she did it!

Cruising into the car yard, where she purchased the vehicle, Susanna had looked around for somewhere to park. Finding no available space, she had left it immediately outside the entrance way to Reception. Walking in, she had then informed the staff member at the reception desk that she had returned the car as per the conversation they had shared five minutes earlier on the phone.

She had been told to wait in the less busy section of the area. So, she waited. She waited some time – everyone seemed busy, so she sat and waited some more, until a very officious and angry senior salesman came storming through the door, yelling, "Madam, you've left your car blocking our driveway. Please move it!"

Susanna had quietly stood up, faced the man and, handing him the keys had said, "Sir, I believe it's your car!"

He had then snatched the keys from her hands and stormed back out of the building.

It was then interesting to Susanna how quickly staff in the reception area hustled her away from the prying eyes and ears of the stunned, confused but slightly amused waiting customers watching her performance. The reception had been very busy, with many people left sitting, waiting to be attended to. This sudden burst of entertainment had made their day, and they applauded her.

Susanna was not in the mood, though, for entertainment. She was here on business.

"Mrs Newth, what makes you think you can return the car?" a female assistant had looked puzzled at Susanna.

Susanna explained the clause in ACL.

"Darling, you can't believe everything you read on the internet."

Returning from moving 'his' car, the over-pompous senior salesman burst once more into Susanna's space, agreeing with his off-sider, had then sneered, "I deal with Fair Trading all the time, and I can assure you our warranty policies have not been breached."

"I'm not talking about warranty," Susanna had simply said, "I'm talking about your guarantee for your product."

The lady assistant at this point had become quite annoyed, frustrated and impatient with her stubborn customer. She was also taken aback by Susanna's perfectly calm and in control demeanour – so unlike any other customer would have been in any similar situation.

"Lady, we can fix the car for you. How will that be?" the senior salesman growled at Susanna.

"I'm not choosing that option. As I explained on the telephone to you earlier this morning, that under ACL, Major Fault Clause, I decide if I want a full refund or repairs. I choose the full refund. I can also expect you to pay the cost of the repairs that were needed to be done yesterday, and I can claim back the petrol I had to purchase, in order to drive the vehicle. You have my personal and bank details, and I expect this in my bank account this afternoon."

Susanna had then left the building, watched every inch of the way by the waiting throng of other dissatisfied customers – well Susanna had assumed they were dissatisfied as they had seemed angry and fidgety as they had all sat waiting to be served.

Yes, the money had appeared in Susanna's bank account that afternoon – and, yes of course the snarly senior salesman had phoned Fair Trading! But...

Susanna had stood her ground that day and won.

In her discussions on the phone with the female assistant later that afternoon, when she had enquired if Susanna had received the refund, it became clear to Susanna that this car yard had not been familiar with the changes to consumer law. The concern this lady now had was whether Susanna was going to follow up charges against the original salesman for 'lying' to her about having had the car checked by mechanics prior to the sale.

Of course, the car hadn't been checked.

And of course, Susanna wasn't going to take the matter further – she had better things to do with her time!

The phone call had ended amicably.

"I'm now reading the ACL fine print," she had said to Susanna, as she had wished her a great day.

I rest my case.

An interesting off-shoot to this scenario was that Susanna had stupidly left her motorway tag in the vehicle. One of the sales team staff members at the car yard had instantly realised this and decided to use it to his advantage. Before reselling the vehicle, he had driven it as his own personal vehicle to and from work for a month, and had then removed the tag, placing it on another car for his personal use for a further two months.

When the car yard and the freeway tag operators had finally caught up with him, he had amassed a bill of in excess of $10,000.

"Ouch!" Susanna had laughed with the saleslady, when she had finally found out which of her staff members had been the culprit.

"And, darling, I'm going to make sure he pays it!" She had laughed with Susanna.

All Susanna knew was that she was glad she didn't have to pay it – all she lost was the $40 cost of the tag.

"Well, it just goes to show – it pays to read 'the fine print'."

Saga 25
A Conversation with a 2-Year-Old

Susanna arrives at her son's house to briefly chat to him. He had been forced to stay home that day to look after his little girl, who was sick. She was just fourteen months old.

Opening the door, the little girl immediately runs up to Susanna and begins a lengthy diatribe, castigating her father for everything he would not let her do that morning. All Susanna and her son could do until she'd finished was watch and listen.

The conversation lasted exactly twelve minutes! Susanna was gobsmacked – the child knew exactly what she was saying, why and the context of the moment – truly amazing to witness! (How can a child who has just learnt to say 'mama', suddenly hold a lengthy conversation about ideas and concepts, many of which many adults struggle to express themselves well orally?)

A few months later Susanna's granddaughter is sitting at Susanna's computer. It is a warm day and so she has decided to take all her clothes off. Susanna's computer is a touch screen, and one that the little girl loves to use to paint her pictures.

Opening up the new Paint program, the child begins her usual artwork.

"Nanny, you do your work on this computer?"

"Yes, darling."

"I not darling – I _____." (She says her name.)

"Nanny, I'm doing work like nanny on the computer."

Susanna watches this little eighteen-month-old sit up at her desk, access both text and painting programs using a mouse and her fingers, with more dexterity than she has seen many school students and certainly many older – technology skilled adults. She wonders how these little beings become so smart so quickly!

2019 just after Easter. Susanna and her granddaughter share a Saturday morning together.

"Nanny, let's do a Wiggle's concert." (Wiggles is a popular children's singing group.)

"Alright. Are we going to do this on the white rug, or in the garage?"

"Silly Nanny. We're going to Anita's Theatre in Thirroul, of course!"

(Anita's Theatre was the venue for the previous Wiggle's concert that the little girl had been to with her cousins.)

"Oh, alright then. Let's go."

The pair get into Susanna's car – the two-year-old at the steering wheel. She puts her seatbelt on.

"Nanny – put your seatbelt on. I can't drive with you not wearing your seatbelt. Here, let me help you."

With Susanna all buckled-up, the little girl checks the lights, checks the mirror, waves to her clan of Wiggles folk all seated (apparently) in the back seats, yells out, "Wake up Lachie!" – looks at Susanna – "He'd fallen asleep, Nanny" – opens the garage doors using the remote, and says, "We're off!"

She then imagines she drives to Thirroul.

"We're there, Nanny."

The child gets out of the car – with Susanna's help.

"Come on, children, sit in these seats here."

The little girl busily organises Susanna's artificially turfed grass area of her garage, transforming it into a stage area with seating for all the children. She then takes Susanna's mobile phone, uses the passcode (hang-on, how did she know this?) and switches on ABC Wiggles.

Standing at the front of her imaginary stage, she plays the perfect compare.

"Ladies and gentlemen, please welcome The Wiggles," and she then proceeds to name each of them in turn.

The compare then plays the first song – 'Wheels on the Bus'.

"Come – on Nanny, we have to be the bus!"

For the entire duration of the Wiggles album of songs (45 minutes) Susanna's granddaughter danced, performed every song in the way that the band did at the concert, got all the children up dancing and singing, and then finally said to her audience, "Ladies and gentlemen, mums and dads, children and babies, please thank the Wiggles!"

She then yanked her nanny back into the car, put her seatbelt on and said, "Home time!"

Amazing concert!

Susanna's granddaughter enjoys going to her nanny's place on Saturdays. She rushes in and hauls herself full pelt at Susanna's arms, trusting that the lady will catch her.

"Mum – look at her. She's so happy to come here. She's so shy everywhere else we go," Susanna's son proudly boasts to his mum.

"Nanny, are you **my** special nanny?"

"Yes, darling."

"But, Nanny, are you only my nanny?"

"No, I have other grandchildren."

The little girl looks dolefully at Susanna.

"Can you show me pictures of my other cousins?"

"How do you know they are your cousins?"

"Because you are my daddy's mummy. He has a sister, and her children are my cousins. Nanny, I know these things."

Susanna thinks, *She gets it! I remember being about six when I understood this family relationship.*

The little girl then looks at her nanny, "Nanny, I miss you so much, when you're not with me."

Going upstairs Susanna's son takes an ice-cream from the freezer. Seeing this, his daughter immediately runs over to Susanna to dob him in.

"Cheeky Daddy, Nanny."

"Thanks, darling," Susanna's son looks at his daughter.

(Susanna thinks, *What she really wants is one too! So cute!*)

A little while later, when Susanna and her granddaughter are alone, they are browsing pictures of babies on the internet. An article catches the little girl's eye.

"Look, Nanny. There's baby _____." (Name withheld)

Susanna scrolls down and reads the article.

"Nanny, that's me when I was a baby. I died." The little girl looks up at her nanny and says, "I had a different mummy and daddy then."

Susanna read the article and her hair stood on end, tingles went through her entire body and she stared unbelievingly at her granddaughter.

The article was about a child who had died at two years of age due to medical complications. The article was written on the child's would be – second birthday – after a chapel had been built at the hospital. (The parents of the child had set about raising funds for a hospital chapel, so that other parents who also lost children to illnesses, had somewhere to use for church services and memorial occasions.)

The child's name was _____. Name withheld – but the same as Susanna's granddaughter – and not a common name.

When this child came into this world, she chose the same name for herself.

How did she know that baby was her?

Susanna had hugged her granddaughter and said, "Darling, you are an amazing little girl."

Saturday morning, quite recently, the little girl arrived as usual and immediately hauled herself into Susanna's lap.

"Nanny, can I come to work with you?"

"Have you been to work with Mummy?"

"No, silly, she's a doctor!"

"Have you been to work with Daddy?"

"No, Nanny – he works in the city."

"So why do you want to come to work with me?"

"Because you are a teacher and you teach children. I'm a child."

The little girl then goes on to explain to her nanny how big she is compared to the children she perceives her nanny teaches. One child is apparently as big as the ceiling, and one child is just a bit bigger than her.

"See, Nanny, I'm this big and your students are this big, so I can come to work with you."

"Alright – one day."

A happy little girl then dances off to play with the toys.

Last conversation

Saturday 17th August 2019

Susanna messages her son that she has lessons now on Saturdays until 11.00am. Susanna's granddaughter usually comes around 10.30am as she's a late riser. She then advised him that she had to do some of her business work for a short while.

When Susanna's granddaughter found out she would be going to her nanny's place a bit later than usual, she called Susanna on the phone.

"Nanny, are you doing your work this morning?"

"Yes, darling, I'll see you later."

Susanna's son had then messaged his mum back.

"She's really upset, so we're going to the shops."

Susanna then taught her lessons and had just finished when the phone rang.

"Nanny, have you finished your work yet?"

"Yes."

"So, I can come now?"

A few minutes later:

"N a n n e e e e y!" a child's voice yells out at the top of her voice.

"Have you finished your work **now**?"

Susanna thinks, *This child wasn't upset that I had to do things, she was downright affronted! How can a two and a half-year-old understand this concept? Hmm! This child is going to be an interesting little girl as she grows up!*

As the pair sat down on the lounge to chat, her granddaughter placed her left eye on Susanna's shoulder. "Nanny, I've got my eye on you!"

Susanna laughs – "That is so cute!"

Saga 26
The Hypocrite

This is an interesting discussion point. Susanna is mulling over the merits of people she has encountered, who have challenged her understandings of this concept. She questions her own ethics and truthfulness, as well as the behaviours of others, and seeks to ascertain if hypocrisy rears its ugly head in any of these scenarios.

Scenario 1:

A female family member on her husband's side was unable to attend a function organised by Susanna, after which Susanna posted four very carefully chosen photographs of the occasion on her social media site. Within half an hour of posting, the female family member replied with the comment, "One doesn't have to attach importance to photos by sharing them with others, as the memories of the occasion are far more important."

This was actually the first time that Susanna had ever shared any of her photos on this site. The photograph on the left is one of the ones she shared that day. It was a momentous occasion – highly worthy of being shared. Her husband was truly 'The Monk'!

The next day, a roll of 25 photos were posted by said person – of her two children on the same social media site. Susanna can only presume that the occasions at which these photographs were taken held no particularly significant importance for this girl or her two boys.

Young Garin of Monglane,
The Last Song of Deeds

Scenario 2:

Susanna had organised a family and friends get together one Sunday. One of her guests had emailed Susanna about providing her with a special meal, as she was vegetarian and sugar-free. Of course, Susanna was more than happy to do this, and had prepared a delicious assortment of vegetables and salads with cheeses. The guest had been delighted, and at the onset of table-talk had professed in length about the benefits of her new dietary plan.

Of course she devoured all portions of her special meal, including the pavlova, cheesecake and chocolate profiteroles afterwards.

What begged the question for Susanna was, "What part of the dessert menu did she think was sugar-free?" (Presumably all of it!)

When reflecting on this memory Susanna is reminded of a scenario at her son's wedding when one of the guests arrived at the reception and immediately demanded a special meal from the proprietors. At no time beforehand had she made any plans to accommodate her needs. Susanna, on the other hand had gone to great lengths to convey her dietary needs beforehand to the establishment. When the dining began, this person was served Susanna's meal – she had actually become aware that it was Susanna's selection of vegetables, but had taken the plate anyway and then smiling at Susanna, had said, "Here, you can share mine!"

Susanna had not been impressed. She continued to not be impressed when the lady helped herself to many of the selections of Vietnamese meats and fish delights that the restaurant had served to all the other guests throughout the night.

Susanna had gone home that night dinnerless and compassionateless!

Scenario 3:

Susanna is travelling to the US to visit her daughter. She has decided to use her airline membership points and upgrade to Premium Economy. As always, she books her vegan meal online directly with the airline.

Settling into her comfortable seat, she relaxes and begins chatting to her co-share passenger. The girl is much younger than Susanna and is returning home. As Susanna enjoys her lunchtime wine (she always allows herself this treat) the girl next to her begins fussing about her food, detailing to the flight attendant that she needs a gluten free meal. Thinking this lady had ordered the salad vegetables, the flight attendant hands her Susanna's meal.

"Mrs Newth, what can I get you for lunch?" a smiling young man peers into Susanna's face.

"Well you tell me!" Susanna smiles back. "Seeing as how **you've** just given my meal to the lady next to me, what do **you** suggest?"

The flight attendant looks troubled, looks across to the companion and then stammers, "I, I'll see if I can find you some fruit." He then hastily heads off to serve other customers, never to be seen again – well at least not for a good two hours.

For those avid zealots, who fanatically read Susanna's sagas know only too well how frequently Susanna is placed in this predicament. She's used to it! She expects it! She takes her own food!

What interested Susanna on that occasion was – the girl next to her had hungrily devoured all of Susanna's meal including the bread, which was certainly not gluten free, as well as an assortment of pastries that had been handed out with the coffee.

The question begs itself again: "At what point did the girl understand that she was eating food she had expressly indicated would do her body immeasurable harm?"

Susanna asks herself the question, "Did the bread and pastries pose any threat to her health and well-being?"

No, of course not!

Yes, Susanna can ascertain that in each of these four scenarios there is a ***modicum*** of hypocrisy.

Now, she thinks, *let's look at the main reason that prompted this saga – Halloween!*

Is it just Susanna, or are more children venturing out in ghostly costumes on this witchy night to grab their bags of sweeties? There certainly were gangs, garbs, spectres, brews and stews of every imaginable description flaunting the streets this year.

"Oh, **hallo**." in case readers you've missed the obvious pun – "**Hallo** again, I know these children," Susanna smiles as she drives home that night. "Aren't these the same ones whose families have expressly requested they not be given lollies as rewards or treats?"

Yes, of course they are out doing what all other children are doing, and yes, of course they eat lollies at home, and yes of course their mothers don't want the world to know they give their children these treats – which means this form of pretence must surely rank high in the realms of hypocrisy!

And, as Susanna smiles to herself again, her phone pings her. Arriving home and checking her phone, Susanna continues to smile, but this time more wryly, "Oh, '**Hallo**!' Susanna's granddaughter has been out **Hallo**weening!"

Of course, she has! And, of course she will eat the lollies – sweet treats on any other occasion are supposedly banned at any time this little girl is in Susanna's house – but hey, we won't care that this is hypocrisy, will we?

Alright, so before Susanna moves on to her own failings, let's consider anything else.

Let's not go down the legal pathway – let's not even do the politics road, she thinks.

Why not?

She doesn't have to answer that question, she only has to read a newspaper, listen to the radio news or watch 'the box' to know just how these eager legals, or sorry pollies behave – and sadly, mostly at the expense of the public purse!

But, yes, let's do delve deliciously into at least one aspect of religion. "No, it's **OK** f**o**lks, I've ch**o**sen **o**ne n**o**ne of **you** belong to!" (Did **yous** all get the beautiful assonance in this last statement?)

"Honestly, I don't think anyone is blame free on this subject. I would not know where to begin – well I would, but I wouldn't have any friends at the end of it – well I don't anyway!" Susanna laughs. "No, mainstream religions, I'll steer clear of them, at least for now," Susanna smirks.

"But, let's have some fun with this one!"

Susanna was the principal of a primary school in an area where many students practised a minority religious observance order.

Susanna can acutely comment that all the children from these families represented exceptional characteristics in model behaviour, attitudes and applications to their studies. She did find some of their belief systems interesting, however, especially pertaining to celebrations.

Susanna, at her weekly assemblies, celebrated their academic successes by rewarding them with certificates, as all other students who excelled in aspects of their learning were equally rewarded, and she always ensured every child attended any school function that was extra, or external, to the regular school curriculum.

However, she made the observation that the families from this identified religious order preferred that the school paid the costs for their children to attend any, or indeed all, such functions, rather than pay for these events themselves (under the guise that their religion prohibited this form of outlay for such occasions).

All this is fine. People can believe as they will. Susanna has never had a discriminatory or racial or religious observance, or disability disagreement bone in her body. But…and this is where she draws the line…

It was the end of the school year. A group of kindergarten children approached Susanna's office to wish her a Happy Christmas and to give her some cards and gifts. Amongst this gathering were a couple of children from the religious order in discussion. Susanna noticed that these two little girls had made Susanna a card during the afternoon session in class – probably because their teacher had organised for all her children to do this.

During the interlude, one of the boys started talking about what he wanted for Christmas. Soon, all the children began enthusiastically telling their principal about the exciting gifts they would soon be receiving from Santa.

"So, you get a gift at Christmas?" Susanna had turned to one of the two little girls, surprise mounting on her face, but trying hard not to allow the overt expression to become too obvious – yes of course they do – stupid question – move on! Susanna had then wished them all wonderful Christmases and closed the school for the year, as she now closes this discussion about others' wrongdoing – to focus on her own.

"So, how do I fair? I don't dare to care – or do I?" She squirms.

Scenario 1:

Water: Susanna frequently exclaims, sometimes quite rudely, that she never drinks water, not even when she runs or swims. Well, this isn't exactly true, she admits. Lovely Margaret recently bought Susanna a bottle of water, which she drank steadily throughout the course of the morning. Susanna had acquired a migraine and had felt giddy. The water had hydrated her and helped her recover, along with the Panadol Margaret had also supplied.

(Why couldn't Susanna have been this organised?)

So, the truth of the matter is: she drinks white wine, green tea, black decaffeinated coffee and the occasional sip of water – all of which are – 'water'!

Yes, this is hypocrisy.

Scenario 2:

Sleep: Susanna regularly laments at her habitual lack of sleep, claiming to only sleep for four hours per night. Well, this isn't exactly true, she admits. Most nights she will sleep from around 10pm – 1.30am and then remain awake for the remainder of the night, but once in a blue moon she will sleep through until around 4am. When this happens, the euphoria Susanna experiences is beyond belief and relief, as the benefits of a good six hours' sleep are blissfully beyond description. Rare as this is, it does happen! So, yes, another example of hypocrisy!

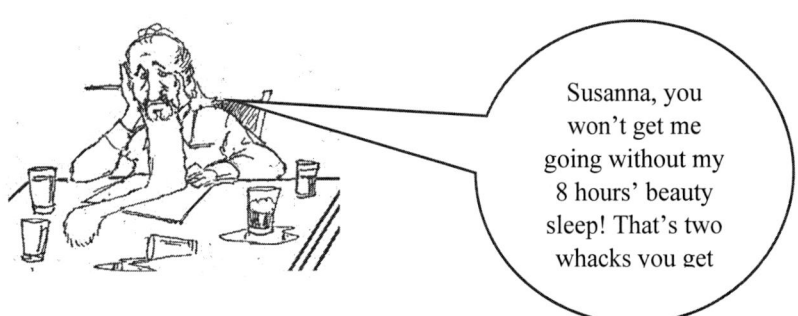

Scenario 3:

Food: Susanna has been vegan in her diet for a good many years, preferring not to eat any foods obtained from any part of any animal. Her family on her father's side were extremely observant Christian Scientists, who lived strict, stringent lives. They went one giant step further than Susanna, by banning any substance, not just food, obtained from any animal.

So, would anyone expect to find foods in Susanna's fridge that are of animal substance?

The simple answer is 'no' but the true answer is 'yes' because Susanna's fridge is not for her exclusive use.

"Ha, ha Gary! You don't get to whack me three times!" Susanna laughs.

- Freezer contains frozen meals left by Susanna's 'Unwelcome Guest'. The freezer also contains the son's ice-creams as well, as his daughter's ice blocks.
- Fridge upper section contains son's energy drinks, chocolate and cans of coke.
- Fridge lower section contains Granddaughter's bread, ham and cheese for her toasties and her juices.
- Side cabinet contains milk for drop-in friends' coffees and any other available space – not much – houses Susanna's wine, sprouts, cabbage, tomato, avocado, onion and potato – all single items as she only needs one of each to last her all week!

Folks, if anyone wants more, there's the 'Hypocratic Hypocrite', the 'Flabby Fight', the 'Yoga Guru' or … you name it – there's a sh _ _ load of it out there!

Saga 27
A Picture of Dorian

Oscar Wilde wrote 'The Picture of Dorian Gray'. Oscar was my husband's favourite literary writer. I thought this was an apt title for this saga given the ominous approach of Dorian.

Hurricane Dorian swept through the Bahamas in August 2019, causing severe damage to this part of the world. It was estimated to travel northwards, encroaching on the Georgia coastline before heading to the Carolinas.

Fortunately for the residents of Savannah, the storm focused its attention on the Bahamas and then became very slow moving as it veered to the right – away from the coastline.

The first part of this saga is a narrative introduction.

Gray watched the plane land. This would be the last plane to land that day as menacing skies forced the last remaining flight in the air to return to base. The state of Florida was in a state, panic sweeping the streets like a pressure bubble ready to explode. Tampa tempers were flaring, patience was wearing thin and supplies in shops were diminishing rapidly as residents rushed to grab what they could before the monster hit.

When it did, it would not be a pretty picture, Gray thought, as he recalled a similar scene three years ago when Matthew left his calling card. "Yes, Dorian is a keen competitor. He's more powerful by sixteen miles per hour, surging his swell along this Florida coastline."

The airport terminal was becoming busy. Others, like Gray, had hoped to escape the storm's wrath, but the hurricane had crept upon them quicker than expected, now holding them prisoners until he decided what to do with them.

There's nothing Gray can do. *At least the airport affords me shelter, if not comfort, except it is some comfort that there is food and water enough until Dorian passes*, Gray surmises. *Others in shelters or battling to batten down their houses, may not be so fortunate.*

As Gray sits watching the plane land, it skids dangerously close to the runway fringes. Fierce gusting winds try to force the little Cesna onto the sodden verges of the grassed area, Gray knew would soon become swampland with heavy rains falling now like sheets of glass.

He chats with his fellow companions. None remember Eloise. She destroyed eight thousand houses along the Panhandle; some remember Bertha and her big tides; few recall Andrew, who was responsible for massive tree devastation from his punishing winds, and all spit venom at their memories of Irma who killed eighty of their closest friends. One thing they all accepted, living in Florida was their private paradise, but it came with a price – hurricane season – the season that put closure on the summer season.

"What's that noise?" a frightened child suddenly screams out and then erupts into a fit of frenzied crying.

Gray moves to hold the child.

"He's here!" a man yells out, but his words are lost in the ether as the sounds of a thousand steam trains roar through the airport terminal. The outside airport lights go out, followed quickly by the internal ones. There's nothing anyone can do except huddle together and wait until their unwelcome guest has gone.

Then, hopefully, they would return to their homes and quietly clean up whatever was left of them. Gray hoped his little shack would still be standing, but he feared the worst.

Susanna watches the progress of the storm with more than just a passing interest. She has a house and a daughter who lives in Savannah – the gateway to America for Floridians. Savannah, once a bustling, busy seaport that welcomed sailors and merchants alike to its shores is an historic town of great historical interest and fascination.

Susanna wonders sarcastically if these annual hurricanes are nature's vengeance on those fortunate folks who reside in this part of the world, who enjoy nine months of perfect beach weather – almost like nature's way of punishing them, "Ha, ha! Take this! I've given you the best of the weather, now let's see how you like the worst!"

The average daily summer temperatures in Savannah this year have been in excess of 110° Fahrenheit coupled with humidity at 100%. (Susanna smirks at whether this weather really is 'perfect', summer, weather conditions!)

Gazing concernedly at the synoptic map, Susanna is drawn to a memory in her not too distant past when she was in Savannah one Sunday afternoon. She still remembers vividly the eerie sound of the steam train that passed her house that day. (Of course, steam trains don't run anymore!) But… they did that day!

The Express Train

The day Susanna thought an express train was about to tear through the entire upstairs of her house is a day she will never forget. It was exactly 3.15pm on a Sunday afternoon when Susanna was busy writing in her study on the second-storey level of the house, and the sky suddenly turned really black. There had been no visual warning of what was to happen.

At any time in the year, this part of the world is susceptible to tornados because the warm air travelling up from Florida to the port of Savannah meets colder, northern air that causes this air to swirl into whirlwinds that then travel up and across the states of America.

On seeing the darkening sky, she moved across to the windows on the left of her study desk. Standing stock still, Susanna then felt goose bumps crawl all over her skin, and the hairs on the back of her neck began to rise with the anticipation of a terrifying event. Within seconds, she had heard the sounds of an approaching express train that thundered across from the right side of her house to the left. Of course, it wasn't a train!

As she looked out of the windows, she was flabbergasted at seeing huge items of furniture being catapulted four metres sky-high, flying past and upwards, until they crashed a few moments later in her back garden. A glass table had been propelled over ten metres high, and on landing on her porch had shattered into a million tiny pieces.

She shuddered as she had thought about what would have happened had she been standing outside, or even driving her car, at the time. She too would have been blown sky high!

Rushing downstairs, she was just in time to see a child's play fort flying at several kilometres per hour smashing into her kitchen windows. The impact of wood on glass was ear-shattering, with dust, glass and debris flying everywhere. Within seconds the whole of the downstairs living areas resembled a war zone.

All Susanna could do was wait until the monstrosity had passed, and then clean up.

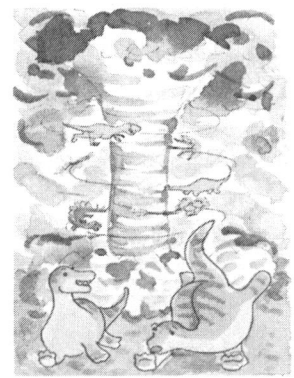

The tornado lasted fifteen minutes, circling at 150 kilometres inside the funnel and 180 kilometres an hour in a forward direction. The initial formation of the circular wind started immediately, the air reached Savannah, and then flew like a circling rocket throughout the entire length of her street, where it promptly went straight back out to sea.

Susanna immediately rushed out into the street to see how much damage had been done outside, and to assist her neighbours, who were all extremely shell-shocked and traumatised.

Susanna had said to them, "We are all okay. Our houses are fine, and we are not hurt."

Almost all the roofs had been blown off, and large flaps of cladding, concrete, wood and bricks lay strewn everywhere. The mess was considerable. The 15-minute devastation took 15 hours to clean up.

She didn't get any more writing done that day, and it had been an incredible sight to witness!

Returning her thoughts back to Gray and his predicament, she shakes her head when she considers, "Why are these people so surprised when the hurricane beast hits? (He does this every year at this exact same time!) Why do they all panic and rush to the shops to stock up? Why do they all leave it so late to make their plans to leave? Florida has one main road that leads northwards to Georgia.

"What is the point in them heading northwards into the mainland, when the beast surges ahead of them on his path northbound?" Susanna smiles wryly, "And so much more cunning – certainly much quicker and undoubtedly more thinking about how much devastation he can make on his journey."

No, Susanna concludes, if it were me, I'd put up the shutters well in advance, batten down the hatches, stock up the pantry with unperishable foods, keep a stash of batteries and torches at hand – and just 'put up' and 'shut up'!

Susanna, as always, the pragmatist!

Saga 28
Loss of Virtue

> This saga was prompted by television debates recently that considered the merits of the Australian Education System. The main issue presented in one of these debates was the sliding literacy levels of many students across Australia.
> Susanna knows only too well how many students struggle to acquire proficiency in reading, writing, spelling and grammar tasks. She also feels remorse that many students will never enjoy 'a good book', preferring instead to rely on their technological toys for their amusement and enjoyment.
> Susanna acknowledges that this saga is based on her 'opinions' and not on statistical data. Her opinions are founded on her fifty years of empirical observation and classroom practice within Australia as well as overseas across a range of educational environments pre-school to Year 12 and beyond.

Over the years, as each generation of children leaves the primary education system, Susanna reflects on the skills these students have mastered. Do they demonstrate better skills than she did when she was at this stage of her learning?

Going back two hundred years in the education system, learning was predominantly rote learning with the belief that students were required to commit to memory large volumes of information. This information included learning spelling words, poems to recite by heart, hymns that were sung, general knowledge facts, mathematical tables and mathematical processes.

The onus of accountability in learning was on the child, with the teacher's job to monitor progress and facilitate the next volume of rotes to be learnt. Children had to be diligent – they had to actively learn their work – fear of failure and shame loomed heavy – fear of humiliation by being made to perform in front of peers forced every child to learn and fear of the cane, from both the teacher and their parents, forged in children an ethos about learning that gave them no choice about their learning pathway.

They quite simply had to become disciplined learners!

Going back just one hundred years, many of the disciplines in education still existed. The methodologies and examination structures were rigid. The 3 Rs held priority place on every daily schedule with children mastering the basics of reading, writing and 'rithmetic by the time they finished primary school.

Many children entering kindergarten could tell the time, read children's books without assistance – teachers did not necessarily have to teach instructional reading – and they knew how to count. Having these base line skills on entering the school system gave teachers a brick wall on which to build further foundation skills, so that children quickly grasped the skills and concepts of higher order learning.

And at this time there were no pre-school programs! There were also no stimulating educational games! Children had to make their own entertainments in their play! There were no computers or televisions or video games or electronic cars or…

There were children's classics to read. There were board games. There were porcelain dolls that sat on shelves, and there were balls to kick around or throw. Going back to 1955 when Susanna entered the school system, she clearly remembers being able to read and write in kindergarten. Every day the class would read stories silently, write diary entries and rote learn tables. They also rote counted forwards and backwards by many patterned numbers and no teacher taught time as a separate skill.

In a recent Year 7 Mathematics test, one task was to find the pattern of this set of numbers: 1: 7: _: 19. Another task was to locate a position on a map in which a house was located on a grid reference C4. (Seriously!)

By the time Susanna left Year 6 she was accomplished in being able to write essays, short stories and poems using correct punctuations and having knowledge of the skills and purposes of grammar. She also had instant recall of all table facts to 12 x tables.

In 2005 Susanna once walked into a Mathematics staffroom in a high school to chat to a teacher. The young, Mathematics teacher began a conversation about learning tables. Susanna threw a couple of easy ones at her '3 x 4' and '5 x 6' and she counted on! (Susanna was flawed!) She then gave her a couple of harder ones, '7 x 8' and '9 x 6' and she could not provide answers. (Seriously!)

So, where is education going?

The simple answer is – it's not!

Australia's external assessment program proves this.

When government primary schools in NSW used to sit basic skills testing in English and Mathematics, the tests did not provide much statistical information about children's results as comparative data. Children were graded. At this time parents accepted this graded system – they wanted to know if their child was an A, B, C, D or E student and they wanted to know the position their child was ranked within their child's school assessment programs. That was in essence, all parents wanted to know, relying totally on the knowledge and skills of the teacher to provide the education, and certainly trusting the outcomes.

When outcomes-based education came in, this graded system was abolished, which upset the parent bodies. The reporting system of student outcomes upset the teachers! They simply did not want to do the work involved in providing individualised programs for children who were not performing at expected standards. So, the outcomes approach was retained but ignored and the grading system came back in!

When these basic skills tests were replaced with the external battery of assessments, that also included the high school arena, many teachers were unhappy about the accountability framework. Now, 20 years later, these assessments are still viewed as unwelcome guests in most classrooms!

Did you know that when the first tests were orchestrated around 2008, Year 3 and 5 sat the exact same tests? Two years later, when the Year 3 students were in Year 5, and sat the exact same test as Year 3, so many of them demonstrated no progress, with many again showing significant declines. It appeared quite significantly that Year 5 students across the state were not making satisfactory gains. (Seriously!)

This was a huge concern for the education system! Now, the tests are structured in such a way that most students can access the average performance bar. The level of extension from this bar, however, does not rise steeply? Why not? Because students must show progress!

Did you know that all potential teachers must now sit basic testing in English and Mathematics? Has anyone looked at these tests? What is the standard?

Susanna would very much like to see the statistical data in respect to the performance outcomes of each cohort of beginning teachers.

A question?

If a teacher passes this test at the satisfactory level, are they equipped sufficiently to teach high school English and Mathematics? Are they equipped to teach capable students – Susanna doesn't use the term Gifted and Talented – she rarely meets too many of them, even when she prepares students for Selective School or Scholarship Programs?

How can the education of children be improved when the skills and knowledge of so many teachers are in deficit?

It really would be an interesting experiment to conduct national testing of teachers – give each of them the Year 7 external examination papers! So, why don't they? Because Susanna feels the system is fearful of the results.

So, my friends, we're back where we started – loss of virtue!

But, hey! Kids talk better on mobile telephones; they are quicker at texting on these phones and they are more adept at using computers and software programs. And, hey again – if they can't spell, the mobile likes their Text-Talk, and Siri does it for them on their computers! So, why bother to learn anything, anyway!

In closing, a word of advice: *Semper ubi sub ubi!*

Susanna wishes she'd learnt Latin – she would have loved it!

Saga 29

'Come on Down!'

> Susanna's blog this week is in response to a query she had regarding an ATAR (the university entrance score) for acceptance into primary teaching. Last week's blog was the loss of virtue in study habits of students, and this blog naturally follows on from this idea.
>
> When scanning the internet, Susanna was amused by the advertising material and strategies used by one university, that will remain nameless, which caused her huge concerns for the future of education.
>
> Readers – believe it or not! This saga is fair dinkum!
>
> Seriously – what is 'f_____' going on?
>
> Susanna rarely actually uses 'that' word – saved only for those 'exceptional' times when no other expletives are sufficient to convey the absolute abhorrence that she has pertaining to the matter at hand – in this case – the teaching standards! How can they get away with this? Who is the regulating body for university standards?
>
> Oh, well readers, you judge for yourselves. A really, fun exercise would be to craft a curly question for your child's teacher when you next meet at a parent/teacher interview. Will they be clever enough to answer it?

Come on down! Let us train you to be a teacher! Great hours, great holidays and great pay incentives if you want to advance your skills once you've become accredited.

So, what do I need to begin the process?

1. Study hard at school?

Nah, we can offer you a course without any ATAR. If you've had family problems and not performed well in school – no worries – we're the ones for you!

2. Save up the course fees?

Nah, we can offer you 75% of your tuition fees paid through government grants with the remaining not required until you begin earning tax – at least 4 years away!

3. Have above average skills in core curriculum subjects I will be required to teach to students?

Nah – don't worry about these trivialities – we have great cafés, bars, outdoor leisure seating, sporting venues and a social club – see here's a group of zealous students relaxing after a hard day of study!

The university site actually shows a group of students drinking coffee, or soft drinks, and playing on their mobiles during the middle part of the day!

4. Know the meaning of pedagogy and methodology?

Nah, don't stress about these words, let alone know their meanings. We don't even include them in our course outline – in fact we don't even include that frightful word 'education' in our course handbook!

5. So, what do you include in your course outline for a Master of Teaching degree?

a. Great computer labs and study areas inside and out

b. Many restaurants and cafés – you get hungry when you study (they really say that!)

c. Many fun electives

d. Some practical work – learning is fun – you can join in and make friends

e. Flexible study timetables – work from home if you want to

6. So, I don't actually have to study Educational Psychology and Philosophy, Educational Methodologies, Methodological Research, Core Teaching Curriculum, Strategic Curricula or Behaviour Management?

Nah! You just need a WWC Clearance number.

7. So, how do I get that?

Pay $82 to the RMS (Roads and Maritime Services) through any Service NSW.

Too easy – when can I start?

As soon as you've paid your money!

Susanna just shakes her head!

Saga 30
The Reading Debate or Debacle

> This saga is in response to the ABC 4 Corners documentary called, 'Digi Kids' aired on Monday 11th November 2019, Sydney, NSW, Australia.

Yes, Susanna has watched part of this Four Corners documentary on 'Reading'.

So, the obvious question pokes her in the eye. Do children learn to read through a phonics approach?

When she studied to become a teacher, she was presented with two sides of the coin:

- whole language v
- decoding strategies

Susanna read widely in her attempts to formulate her own opinion. Clearly reading is not decoding! Decoding is the sounding out of regular words that conform to the rules associated with the 44 phonemes in the English language. Sounding out can be a useful process in establishing what the decoded word is, so that it can then be read correctly. Having been read correctly, can then be transferred into the reader's memory banks for recognition at other times.

Whole language approaches are about teaching students to see the whole word. This approach does not consider any phonemic structure and does not promote the connection between graphemes and phonemes.

What concerns Susanna currently is the lack of understanding and certainly knowledge that many teachers have about 'why' they teach the strategies they employ. Even in the documentary, Susanna cringed when she saw the rote learning approach for a couple of the spelling rules and sounds. One of the sounds the students were articulating was 'wh' as 'w/h' – separate sounds with the stress on the 'h' sound, when sounded out at the beginning of a word.

No, we don't say, 'w/hen' nor do we say 'w/here' – rather the sound is clearly 'w' with the 'h' as silent. (Perhaps we are supposed to sound out both letters, but do we?)

We teach students that many consonants and vowels walk with partners who do the talking!

The next phoneme was the sound the 'ew' (oo) makes at the end of a word. Is it always 'oo'?

No. We can teach the sounds that letter constructs (graphemes) make, but…

We must also teach the words that don't follow that sound. In this case we have the constructs of 'sew, sewn, sewing, sewed'. There is also the word 'ewe' which has a similar construct but has the beginning consonant 'y' sound.

The teacher was teaching this 'ew' sound at the end of words. But… is it an 'oo' sound at the end of a word. Words like 'new, few, stew' all have the 'yew' (you) sound.

If the letters 'ew' are placed in the middle of a word, as in 'crewel' or 'lewd' is the sound the same? No, in these cases the sound is a definite 'oo' sound.

So, what if two vowels go walking, as in these words, 'view, preview, purview?' Is one of these vowels silent, do they both make one sound or is the 'i' a diphthong? The 'i' is a diphthong as the sound slides into the 'y-oo' sound.

Was this mentioned in the video? No.

If we teach students the sounds that graphemes make, we are doing so primarily for reading purposes as the teacher was doing in her classroom in the video. What is the difference when teaching graphemes for spelling purposes – many commercial educational resources introduce spelling programs with this strategy. Do teachers question this approach? No, because they don't know how to do it!!! They rely on the program, which doesn't do it because it's the wrong approach. (I can't say this with any more passion, and I'll be saying it on my death bed – we learn to spell by firstly – 'listening to the sounds that letters and syllables make'. We then make the correct letter/sound grapheme choice. If students have access to all the spelling choices, their brains select the correct choice because their visual memories have remembered it!!!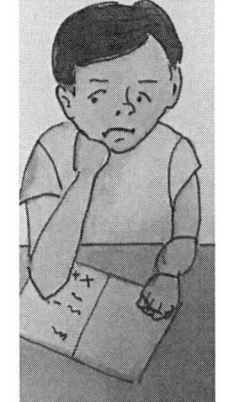

It is so simple – why is it such a debacle?

Because so many teachers teach spelling by giving their students words to learn by rote (which is a strategy that went out decades ago) and then test them as a visual memory strategy. Only applying this visual memory approach, does not teach students to look at words afterwards and check to see if they are spelt correctly. What it does is to detract from teaching that!

The Reading and Spelling Process

Reading is the conversion of graphemes into phonemes. Spelling is the conversion of phonemes into graphemes.

When reading a word, children need to know the sounds that the individual letters and syllables make. If they don't know the word, they can sound out and make it make sense. Too easy!

In Kindergarten children learn that 'a' has the short vowel sound of 'a' – perfect. Now, let's decode our first story shall we!

"I want a glass of water." (Susanna actually watched a lesson that did exactly this!) How stupid was that – the teacher should only have selected a story that had 'a' sounds, if the task was to decode. This is an example of a teacher who did not know what she was teaching and how, and certainly had not prepared the lesson adequately.

But, Susanna, isn't this exactly what we're seeing in schools at the moment?

Yes, Hippo. Teachers look after our students very well. They make their lessons much more fun than they were in my time at school. They do not give them harsh punishments for making mistakes and they give them goodies for good work. Oh, good-oh!

If the system, though, whatever it is, does not make the students better than Susanna was when she left school, then something is not working, because the education that Susanna received was far from the best, and yet in today's society she is clearly in the elite sector within the realms that she now operates within – scary thought!

A comment on the 4 Corners program was a concern one lady had about the percentage of students entering the workforce with low literacy levels, and the non-availability of unqualified work. This is already having ramifications. TAFEs and universities are passing students who do not meet the requirements because they need the funds and don't want to face a rebuttal. We are seeing employees writing poor-quality emails, sending out incorrectly spelt, structured and punctuated letter correspondence, and answering queries in oral language forms without full knowledge of correct oral language constructs.

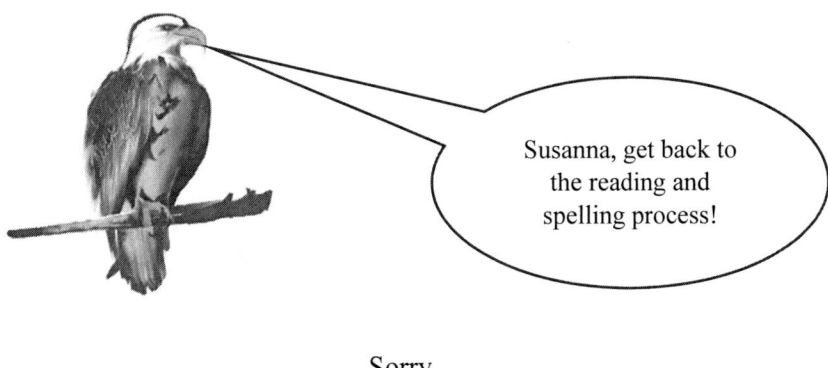

Sorry.

The single 'a' has nine different recognisable sounds. So, when a child is reading, he/she needs to know these sounds to make sense of the word, or the decoding process does not make sense.

This means teachers must teach these sounds early on in Kindergarten at the same time they focus on teaching the short vowel sounds. They teach their children that the vowels have changing sounds. When decoding, the teacher makes sure that only short vowel sounds are decoded at this stage of the children's reading development. All other words are learned as sight words: was saw all day any are car bare calm quay polar.

Once children are beginning to learn the regular sounds and have begun to develop a word bank in their brains of sight words, they can then be taught to find the patterns. The more children find their own patterns, the better they will remember these constructs. (Susanna looked at a core bank of sight words for Kindergarten recently. It contained 20 words in total and included many vc and cv words that were regular. What the f _ _ _! Don't teachers even know the basics? Is this seriously the expectation at the end of Kindergarten? Children are little sponges – they soak up everything that's fed them. How can they, if they aren't properly fed?

So, to teach the patterns:

The teacher asks the question?

When is the 'a' an 'o' sound?

When it is preceded by a 'w'.

Is this always the case?

No, not if the letter 'r' is placed after the 'wa' as it then becomes an 'or' sound.

So, let's make it easy and fun for our children to learn.

Another question prods Susanna in the back. Do teachers know the difference between teaching the 44 phonemes of the English language and the grapheme structures of sounds? "Is this the same thing?" you might ask.

Do teachers know what the 44 phonemes are? Or... is this cause for discourse?

In the 4 Corners program, the word 'diphthong' was shown in large print to represent a phonics approach. The question now on Susanna's lips is:

"If you asked any teacher in NSW what this is, how many would be able to give a clear and concise definition?"

Susanna was amused, when watching the 4 Corners program, that a high school English teacher (not a beginning teacher) openly put herself into the limelight. Her inability to express herself in fluent, cohesive English was poor, she openly admitted to having no knowledge of any grammar, made derogatory judgments about her students' English skills because they couldn't spell a couple of difficult spelling words, and then identified the main area of need in grammar teaching to be that of teaching the apostrophe, left Susanna feeling that there is something savagely wrong in education today. Do teachers actually know what grammar is?

Grammar is syntax and parts of speech.

Punctuation is punctuation.

Too easy Tiger:

- o Educational institutions – schools and colleges need to critically analyse the issues pertaining to their environments. Teacher training courses must teach their students how to teach. Susanna worked for Staffing (DET) at Blacktown for 4 years as an interviewer for the Graduate Recruitment Program. Every beginning teacher is required to go through this interview process.

One of the questions, a Beginning Teacher is asked is, "Identify the steps you take when writing a unit of work."

Susanna would look at them gobsmacked when they couldn't provide an answer.

They don't know what I'm talking about! she would think horrified to herself.

Another common question asked is, "Identify a stage of a student's learning and outline your expectations of the skills in either, literacy or numeracy, that you would expect that student to be able to do by the end of that stage."

"Oh, you don't understand the question?"

"This is core business!" Susanna would cringe.

After some explanation of the task, a common response was, "I'll talk about Early Stage 1. In literacy children can read."

"Anything else?"

"No, of course you don't know – that would be unrealistic for me to expect that a teacher, newly qualified as a Master of Teaching with a 4-year degree has absolutely no capacity to craft an educational program in literacy or numeracy in order to teach the required skills at an identified stage of a student's learning.

"Please excuse the expletive – but… This is the f _ _ _ _ _ _ core of the problem! Too often teachers rely on commercially written programs to do it for them."

"Who writes these?" Susanna asks.

Some are written by practising teachers, others by retired teachers and others who write for a living but are not trained or practising teachers.

- School educational systems – government and non-government systems must critically analyse the programs and teaching strategies they employ and seriously challenge the effectiveness of each strategy, particularly in literacy and numeracy areas.
- School educational systems must make their teaching staffs more accountable for their outcomes. Many teachers still teach behind closed doors, teach whatever they choose to engage students in and blindly refuse to ignore all their employers' attempts to force them to do what they are actually paid to do. (How does Susanna know this – because she was a senior teaching consultant and school principal!)
- All teachers need to upskill their knowledge of English skills – you cannot expect students to learn these skills when the teachers cannot demonstrate their own knowledge and proficiencies. On-line courses can be introduced for every teacher to complete annually.
- Review processes for teacher competency must be implemented in a meaningful way. If teachers cannot show competence in their core classroom practice – then they are not fulfilling their professional obligations. Susanna cannot disclose how often she hears teachers saying things to students that are not correct.
- External assessment data be used as a mandatory tool for tracking student progress. With advanced systems in technology now in place in schools, every student's individual profile can be identified, with their results tracked along the assessment pathway. This would identify any area of neglect and ensure the deficit was addressed.

When watching the 4 Corners program, what really alarmed Susanna was the admission that no one really knows what to do about the problem. Politicians and professors have been identifying a sliding scale of decline in literacy skills for decades but place a resolution approach to addressing the issues in the too hard basket, and so the slide continues.

The program identified that throwing grammar out was like throwing the baby out with the bath water, but Susanna prefers the simile, like throwing the baby's poo out with the bath water, because educational experts have 'poo-pooed' this notion for years!

Saga 31
Restaurant for One!

> This final situational saga puts closure on a chapter of stories, written for entertainment purposes. Readers should form their own opinions about many matters presented in these scenarios, and to share with Susanna in seeing 'the lighter side' of life. This saga is dedicated to her husband.

Susanna sips her usual much-earned glass of bubbly after a long day of writing and teaching. The cat, which isn't her cat, has gobbled up the last remaining portions of ham and cheese saved for Susanna's two-year-old granddaughter.

"Is she so desperate for company that she allows the cat from across the way to sneak in and take up the best seat in the house?" she asks herself as she watches him feast away on his nightly treats.

Apparently, yes! He does this every night. After munching his way through his bowl of delicacies Bobby, the cat, stretches out on the velvety-soft suede lounge to enjoy the warmth and ambience of the gas heater. Within seconds the cat is snoring loudly, and Susanna is left wondering at the merits of the company he is supposed to afford her.

Well the only thing that's being afforded, Susanna thinks, *is the cost of the best ham off the bone slices Bobby has just scoffed, and the detritus of cheese and crackers he has left splattered all across the parquet flooring of the kitchen.*

"Bobby, you really have to go as I'm going to bed!"

Cat snarls at Susanna!

"If you don't leave now, I'm going to fetch your mother!"

Cat looks crossly at Susanna and reluctantly heads off downstairs to the front door.

Like all the children that Susanna teaches, and has taught over the years, Bobby has learnt not to argue with her!

As Susanna once more sits sipping the last remaining bubbles in her glass, she reflects on how her lovely husband used to wait until he heard the garage doors opening, and then quickly pour his equally lovely wife a glass of her favourite vintage, leaving it perfectly positioned on the kitchen counter ready for her arrival.

Such was this ritual every night. Susanna has always sought the pursuits of teaching – even after retirement, unlike her husband who had exited his teaching realm at the earliest opportunity.

He had enjoyed his retirement. He still had his translations, his music, his walks and his garden, but his greatest pleasure was in playing at Susanna's restaurant for one, which he did as his wife enjoyed her first of two daily glasses of sparkling white wine.

Seated at his ivory-coloured piano that took prime position in their open lounge-room area, the musician carefully selected an assortment of classical pieces to play for his one and only dinner guest.

The table would be laid: 1 set of cutlery, 1 dinner plate, 1 napkin all resting neatly on one place mat. The table, an old, oak oblong-styled piece with four matching chairs adorned the dining space and situated facing the musician. Yes, Susanna faced the music every night of the week! And she loved it!

The music was just for her!

Dinner was just for her!

The restaurant was just for her!

How privileged was she?

Susanna's husband was a good musician. Towards the latter stages of his life he had preferred to play the more classical-style pieces unlike his earlier years when he would entertain the masses with his Elton John renditions.

The husband also played the ukulele and saxophone. One time at the school that both Susanna and her husband taught at, they had formed a band known as 'Moving Fixtures'. The musician played both the piano and saxophone in the band, and Susanna was part of a three-some of backing singers, plus played a little guitar. (Well, the guitar was the right size, but she only played it occasionally!)

The female students had loved their concerts, swooning after the male performers, as if they were famous rock stars. (And of course, the rock stars had rocked to the tunes of the day, loving every ounce of attention!)

"Those days are long gone now though," Susanna reflects, as she picks up a school magazine the husband had kept of that era.

His era had started in 1973 when he had been appointed as the language teacher at the school. When he wasn't teaching French or German, he was required to teach sewing to the girls. Not knowing quite what to teach them to sew, he began by taking in his cricket trousers for the class to alter for him. The instructions were to shorten each leg by two inches.

After several weeks of becoming quite absorbed in this special task asked of them, the girls finally showed their teacher the results. He wasn't impressed!

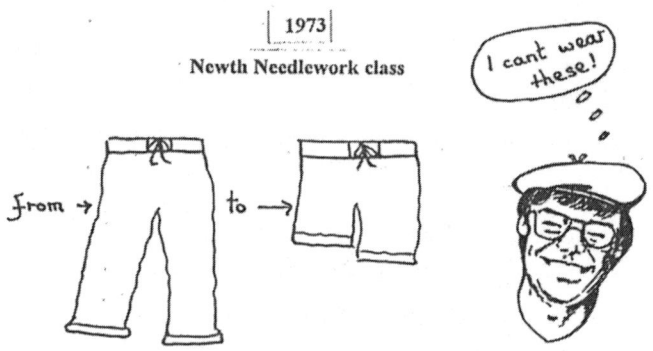

In 1973 the school had a very strict principal. Not many teachers were game to quip with this lady!

Whilst entering the music room one day, the lady had said to the errant teacher, whose class had locked him out of the usual entry point – the door: "Mr Newth, in this school, it is customary to enter a classroom via the door."

"Thank you, Principal, I'll remember that next time," he had smiled sweetly at her.

The next day, the lady had seen the even more errant teacher arriving at school late.

"Late again, Mr Newth!"

"You too, Principal – we really must get up earlier!"

The lady had not been amused!

9/9/74: Susanna had just arrived in Sydney and received her appointment notice to the school where the musician was teaching. As she had walked in the door of the administration building, she had seen a gentleman standing by the office section. Turning to the teacher who had accompanied her, Susanna had said, "That's the man I'm going to marry!"

"Oh, do you know Michael Newth?" The lady had turned and stared at Susanna.

"No, I've never met him," Susanna had simply replied.

They married on 22/12/1979.

To impress his wife to be, the musician took his wife to Noumea – they speak French there. Little did he know that Susanna had spent much time living in France and had spoken very good French – far more colloquially than he could. Sitting in a local restaurant on the first night, the pair had ordered some white wine.

Susanna had sniggered to herself – she still sniggers when she thinks of this incident – when the waiters brought the wine, served in little vinegar pots, the musician had immediately poured his liberally all over his chips.

At this point, Susanna had seen the waiters standing at the bar opening laughing at this gallant act. Susanna had said nothing and had left her vinegar pot untouched for a few moments.

Feeling thirsty, the musician had summoned a waiter, "Garçon, où est le vin?"

The waiter replied, stifling a giggle.

Excusez-moi, monsieur, mais vous venez de le verser sur vos frites!

He had then openly burst out laughing.

Poor Romeo! He never got over that one!

Another incident he was never allowed to forget was when a new principal was appointed to the school. This lady was keen to implement Japanese and had organised for a large contingent to visit the school. Herr Newth had been instructed to do the opening address in Japanese.

"*Kore wa bossu desu,*" Herr Newth introduces the Principal. (The Japanese snigger.)

"Oh, Michael, I do hope you've said something nice about me," the Principal looked across at him a little confused.

"Yes, Principal," he had smiled back.

Literally translated means: 'This **thing** here is the Principal!'

This lady was a rather large lady.

Herr Newth went on to say in Japanese that 'she is very big in education'.

That wasn't the literal translation of what he said – because this time the entire audience of Japanese visitors burst out laughing.

This time the Principal knew that something was wrong and looked even more puzzled at her smiling French/German teacher cum Japanese host.

When Michael asked his co-worker, whose Japanese was much better than his, what he had actually said, she had informed him that he had called her a 'big, fat lady'!

Needless to say, Michael endeared himself to the Japanese throng, and they came back every year for more entertainment!

Moving Fixtures Staff band
1994

This weekend marks the first anniversary of Michael's passing. Not a day goes by when I don't talk to him or miss him terribly. He was 'my musician'!

To all my readers – that's me in the background to the left of Michael. I had a black T-shirt on!

9/8/19

Saga 32
All Things Spiritual

> *This epilogue section provides an insight into the senses that make up our holistic bodies. Susanna is a spiritualist and has come to understandings about how life works through her own personal experiences.*
> *This section is not designed to promote spirituality, nor attempt to persuade others to believe what she believes. It is an account of real-life incidents that have formed the framework of her beliefs.*

Each of us has many senses. Apart from the five anatomical senses of taste, touch, smell, hearing and vision, we also have a sixth sense – a sense of knowing things, without necessarily 'knowing' them.

Susanna is not a practising psychic, even though she is frequently asked to provide intuitive readings for people who want to explore their future options in life. Yes, she can read people like a book. Yes, she can literally see right through people and delve deep into their minds to interpret what they are thinking, but no, she does not have the ability to call upon people's spirit guides in order to communicate with people who have left the Earth plane, and nor can she visualise messages shown to her by any apparitions or spectres.

The type of communication ability that Susanna possesses, she knows has been given to her for a very specific reason, and that is – to share her knowledge with those who seek answers.

We all come to this Earth for a reason. The poem at the front of the book 'Privileged Lives' was written to help people understand that, if we come only for one lifetime, then our lives would serve no purpose. What would be the point in coming to learn lessons, if these lessons did not lead to increased learning for a purpose in our future in whatever realm or eon this may be?

The human body consists of two elements. We have a physical body and we have an ethereal soul. When we die, we leave our physical body behind rather like a snake shedding outworn skin. Our ethereal soul then travels Home. Home is where we come from – we don't come from Earth.

Earth is a tough place. It teaches us hard lessons. This life that Susanna has chosen for herself in this lifetime is particularly challenging. In 2012 she wrote a book entitled 'Tears on the Inside'.

Tears on the outside fall to the ground and are gently washed away. Tears on the inside fall on the soul, and stay, and stay and stay…

By the time Susanna was six years old, she had been physically and sexually assaulted in excess of a dozen times. By the time she was thirteen she had clocked up a few more serious assaults from unknown assailants, intent on doing her harm. By the time she was eighteen years old, she had amassed too many incidents to count. At this time, it seemed to her that it was a lesson she had to learn. So, learn she did.

She accepted it… She learned self-defence techniques… She became the one to **be** feared… At no time in her life has she ever 'played the victim'.

"We all make our own choices as to how we choose to respond," she has stated to many people throughout her life. "I have never sought counselling as a means to understanding the reasons for these incidents, but I have investigated learning about my soul's journey in order to live my life in this lifetime with greater awareness of who I really am and the purpose of my visit here."

"Yes," Susanna smiles, "I chose hard lessons to learn. Some people choose easy pathways, but they don't learn as much. I'm not here to waste time!"

The Gift of Suffering

We enter the world
Upside down,
And journey through life
Backwards.
We cannot know what
Lies ahead,
As this would destroy
All purpose.

We suffer pain
To understand
How to grow in soul,
And strength.
So, treasure hardship –
Welcome strife
And celebrate your
Journey.

We only see where
We have been.
The mistakes we've made
Are clear,
As we survey each
Passing glance
In our journey's path
Through life.

God selects each gift
With great care,
To help and guide us
With love.
Rejoice when times are
Troublesome,
And know His gifts were
Special.

Evidence of the Spirit World

This section is written in first person, as the incidents are of a very personal nature.

In my life I have experienced many episodes that evince the presence of spirit. I have seen visual representations, heard audio messages, channelled for others and felt spirits eye-gouging me or running their hands down my face. None of these incidents have ever frightened me, rather they have fascinated me. I would like to share these three incidents with you.

Incident 1

1988 – Approaching a Give Way intersection, I didn't stop and didn't look right. I only looked left, as I had become disoriented. I'd never driven this way before. My manual car was in second gear as I crossed the white line to turn and enter the very busy main highway. Almost instantly, a large man's face and hands appeared on my windscreen, pushing my car back behind the line. At that exact moment a semi-trailer whooshed past – it would have killed me in a split second.

Afterwards, sitting in my car, I was in disbelief: the car was in second gear, stationary, hand break still off, my feet both firmly planted on the bottom of the car and the engine purring beautifully. How can that be? The image of the spirit form who had saved me, disappeared immediately I was safe.

The man's face, I didn't know at the time, but now do, is my spirit guide – Ahman. I have since met Ahman on several other occasions, these incidents I will relay as part of other sections of this saga. The face and hand I saw on my windscreen covered almost the entire screen, and I could see every detail of his face as if he were peering directly into mine in physical form. As I put my foot on the clutch, placed the car in first gear and drove carefully into the left turn, this time looking to the right, as well as to the left, I knew that this spirit guide would always be with me. To save me at this time, meant that my lifetime in this realm, now, is a significant lifetime for me. Spirit only intervenes in exceptional circumstances.

Incident 2

1991 – A student at the school I was teaching at suffered heart attacks from the time she entered high school in Year 7. She was one of my dancers and was a little angel. Despite numerous visits to doctors and specialists, no one was able to fathom what was wrong with her. When she had an attack, I was always just passing – it was uncanny.

One day her history teacher carried her unconscious and not breathing body across the school to the administration building. I was just entering the building to collect something, when he placed her on a bench and just looked at me – he spoke no words. I immediately conducted resuscitation techniques on her until she came around. I could feel during this process that she was talking to a higher body – that she was in a very deep Theta state.

That night she wrote me a letter explaining what she had discussed with her spirit guides. I answered her family's questions at her funeral a week later. On the day she passed, four days later, she was in control of her time of passing. She waited until her last family member had arrived to say goodbye before she left. She then spent all the next day talking to me – I channelled her wishes and communications to her mother.

This experience was amazing.

When I arrived at her mother's house to set up the channelling session, the door of their house just opened as if they were expecting me – I hadn't told them

I was coming. Fiona had told them! She was 12 and the most perfect spirit I have ever met. I would never have gone to her mother's house – she was my children's principal and teacher!

We learn so much from the passing of a child! Fiona had cardiomyopathy and knew she was too weak for a heart transplant. She came to teach us lessons we couldn't learn any other way.

Incident 3

2007 – My husband's mother had passed suddenly from a heart attack. On the day of her funeral, I had felt waves of electricity running strongly through my veins all day from early morning until 12.47 that night. I initially assumed it was due to the intense heat of summer, as well as from the long drive to the family house four hours south of Sydney. My sixth sense, however, told me it was really, psychic energy. My husband's mother, Mary, had been with me all day. Why she chose me, I don't know – but she did!

Arriving home late, and feeling exhausted, I had gone to bed around midnight and instantly fallen asleep. It was only a short while later, when something woke me up. I felt intensely parched – I'm never thirsty – I never drink water, and I never wake up in the night to fetch a drink. As I lay there, though, feeling the streams of electricity pouring through my veins, I knew I was in the presence of psychic energy.

Looking across at my bedside clock, it read 12.47. I left the room to fetch some water from the kitchen downstairs. On the landing I checked both my children's rooms to make sure my children were sleeping soundly before making my way downstairs.

It was on the third step of the stairs, that something happened. I had felt a momentary shift in consciousness – I can't explain it any other way! It had been a fraction of a second during which time I had felt slightly giddy but thought nothing of it at the time.

I had then continued to the kitchen and opened the fridge door. As I did so, I noticed the oven clock read 1.47, but dismissed this as a possible power cut occurring during the day as a result of the intense heat – it had been over forty degrees Celsius all day.

Pouring some water into a glass, and then turning to carry it upstairs, I noticed the wall clock also read 1.47. Again, I dismissed this, believing this time that my bedroom clock was wrong.

You cannot imagine how I felt as I walked into my bedroom and saw that my clock now read 1.48! How can that be? I'd lost an hour of time on that third step. As I climbed back into bed, drank my water and began to reflect on the events that had just occurred, I knew that Mary had been with me. She had come to make sure I would look after her boy.

The conversation had lasted an hour of Earth time, and then she was gone – so too were the streams of psychic energy I'd felt all day.

Past Life Regression

To experience a past life regression is expensive and so the thought of this indulgence was beyond my financial means most of my married life. It was only when I was plagued with on-going severe neck pain, that I sought this form of hypnosis treatment, as nothing else any doctor had tried had been successful.

2004 – I underwent the first past life regression. I had no idea what to expect and so obeyed every instruction to the letter.

I find myself initially in a beautiful garden of trees and flowers that border a large sandstone building. Here I step gingerly down steep stairs that lead to a courtyard. The air is chilly as I venture towards a cascading waterfall, the sounds of the delicious water enticing me to drink.

I stand under the waterfall and let my body become one with the cascading water until I'm floating on the surface of a large, fast flowing river where I am quickly swept several metres to where the river bends sharply to the right. Turning into the bend I suddenly find myself becoming a young boy of about eight years old. My name is James, I'm wearing grey shorts, a white shirt, a rather scruffy brown jacket, an even scruffier type of brown beret and I'm riding a bicycle along a narrow country lane. I'm riding on the right side of the road as I approach a farmhouse. (I am in France.)

Here a farmhand greets me and leads me towards a paddock, where a horse is waiting, saddled, for me to ride. The man lifts me onto the horse, who immediately rears up, flinging me over the fence to land on my neck. I am killed instantly.

I know that this life was not my most recent one, but probably the one just prior to that one. When the session concluded, I felt great relief in my neck, and have not experienced any neck pain since.

2010 – I underwent a second past life regression, this time to seek answers. There had to be a reason why I experienced an incredibly difficult childhood – a childhood that was plagued with sexual and physical assaults as well as daily bullying taunts. By the time I was fifteen years old, I was so emotionally affected by the on-going abuse, that I seriously contemplated committing suicide. This story is told in another set of sagas entitled 'Looking Back Without Anger'.

On this occasion the hypnosis therapist's house was being renovated and was very noisy. It amused me that I was doing something so un-normal within an environment that was so 'normal'.

Sitting comfortably, I know what to expect this time, and so quickly slip into a deep Alpha state. Immediately I find myself floating through clouds. As I soar upwards, two guides fly down fast to meet me and take me on a journey, one either side of my body.

The first life they show me is that of a happy little girl sewing clothes on a loom with her grandmother. The elderly lady is very plump, is wearing a servant's outfit with apron and her hair is tied in a bun at the back of her head. She is a happy lady, who laughs and tells me stories. The scene is in a large kitchen area, where I can smell the cooking of freshly baked cakes. We both spend the afternoon drinking tea and eating cakes.

The second life I am shown is where I see myself as a young man of twenty-four years old. My name is James and I am wearing a brown pin-striped suit. As I look down from the cloudy realm that enshrouds me, I see James pacing the parkway pavements unsure of what to do. He strides fast from one side of a bridge to the other, looks down at the fast-flowing waters of a river and then gradually lowers himself into its currents.

At the point of facial impact of water, I feel the water gurgling down my throat and into my lungs. I feel my lungs filling up until I feel as if my lungs will explode. This surge of water forces my body to submerge until I slowly sink downwards. At the point of death, I feel a euphoria as my soul is released. (I can still feel this drowning sensation today!)

In that session, I am shown four more scenes, two in which my lives were happy and two in which I found myself committing suicide because of the terrible deeds that had been inflicted on me. The message from my guides was quite clear – you have experienced happy lives, but you didn't achieve much as a result of easy lives. When you were given the opportunities to learn hard lessons, you failed by opting out. In this life now, you have overcome that challenge and have learned valuable life lessons that you will never have to learn again.

2016 – I underwent a third past life experience with the same hypnotherapist but knew that this would be my last with her, as she was moving to Scotland the following week. This session was to find answers to help me understand the pathway my husband and I had chosen for ourselves.

I have always known that my husband and I were soul mates and that we had planned how we would live our lives together in this lifetime. Michael came to translate the Old French manuscripts from the 10th to the 14th centuries into poetic English, almost all of which had never been translated before, and certainly not in sonnet style format. All other translators of this genre have presented their works as prose transcripts. In recognition, Michael was awarded an Honorary Doctorate – Doctor of Letters from Macquarie University in 2012. He was so proud of this achievement. However, once the last book had been published, and the book signing event had been held, Michael had left. He had done what he had come to do.

In the regression session I was taken immediately to the Portal – that entry into the spirit realm.

I am floating upwards towards a cluster of lights. As I approach the Portal, many people come into view, none of whom I know. They are peering into my face, some smiling and some with deadpan expressions. Suddenly Michael explodes forth, brushing all the other entities away until only he remains to greet me. He smiles broadly and embraces my entire body with his arms. He kisses me and calls my name – a name only he knows me by! He then begins talking incessantly about how wonderful this place is, how much I'll like it and how he has been longing for this moment.

When my session ended, I chatted to the therapist about how it was possible for our souls to be in two places at once. At that time, on that day, Michael was still alive, but his cancer was encroaching. Seeing him in the spirit realm gave me great hope for him, as well as for me. It affirmed that we come to Earth for specific experiences. We plan our lives with our guides prior to being born, and when our objectives are achieved, we return home.

Not everybody achieves their objectives in their lifetime. I know this. Some lessons take many lifetimes to be learnt.

So, how is it that our souls can be in two places at the one time?

Our soul – our higher self – always remains in Home. We live within the spirit realm in clusters of like souls. When we come to Earth, or any other planet, we do so for a purpose. We choose the people who will come with us each time and we set our challenges with our guides to make sure we learn the lessons we need to learn. Our guides are always with us to guide and help us throughout our life's journey.

When we incarnate, we decide how much energy we will bring with us. If the life is likely to be particularly challenging, we may choose to bring a higher quota of energy. It is normal to bring about thirty percent, with the remaining energy continuing our life in the spirit realm. At any time, we can call on our higher self – we can acquire more energy if we feel we might need it – people who do meditation may do so specifically to connect to their higher selves during this time, or they may do so to communicate with their spirit guides.

In my husband's case, he brought thirty percent of his energy into his life with me, allotted another thirty percent to another soul who is still journeying through his life now, and the remaining forty percent residing at home. This other 'soul' reincarnated eight years before Michael did. In studying the parallels in both these gentlemen's lives, it is interesting to note:

1. They lived very close to each other as young children growing up in England and experienced very similar childhoods.
2. They both came from working class family backgrounds but were offered musical scholarships on entering high school. This gave them an advantage when studying music, as without such a scholarship to a grammar school, neither of them would have pursued careers in music.
3. Both men became very accomplished musicians, playing the piano, guitar and other instruments. Both were given good singing voices – Michael was the first head choir boy of the new Coventry Cathedral. He was always so proud of being the one chosen to sing for the Queen at the Cathedral's opening service.
4. Both men have identical personas – they have similar natures and personalities.

5. Both men are in the elite field of what they chose to accomplish. One became famous financially and one academically.

In studying the differences, it is interesting that each of these two men chose to experience different aspects of the same lessons they needed to learn. I'm not going to elaborate on this out of respect for the other person, except to say that there would be no point in the soul experiencing the same situation. One man became the carer of his wife who passed with cancer and Michael became the one to experience the cancer. My research links several other facets that show how these two souls are connected and how each aspect of their combined higher self has chosen to learn the lessons they have come to learn.

Life Between Lives

> It is incredible to understand that we can regress into realms we did not know existed. Too often people refute what they don't understand. There is no evidence that our souls do not exist once our physical bodies have died. On the other hand, there is a plethora of evidence (visual, auditory, sensory) that our souls journey Home at the end of a lifetime on Earth. This understanding can be reached through visiting 'Home'.
> Yes, we can go there!
> This last section of this saga describes two occasions when I journeyed into the spirit realm.

The first occasion I sought to enter the spirit realm I was unsure of how this process worked. I was well practised at undergoing the hypnosis to regress into past physical lives, but a novice at this technique.

The first difference I noticed was that I didn't go as deep into a hypnosis trance as I had for all the past life regressions. To enter this spirit realm, I was not required to go into the deep Alpha state, whereas I was expecting to go much deeper, in fact into a deep Theta state.

The regressionist took me immediately into my mother's womb, where I could hear my mother's heart beating, feel the warmth of her body and hear the gurgling sounds of water moving around me. I remember feeling safe and comfortable.

Within a second of feeling this emotion I am standing in a building facing a lift. I'm told to press the number 7 button. The lift takes me to Level 7, where the doors open. Facing me I see the same two guides that I saw in my second past life regression. Ahman is my main guide. He is very tall and has dark hair and a beard. Ali is much shorter and plumper, standing just a few centimetres taller than me.

Both guides embrace me. Ahman looks at me and smiles, "Susanna, you know what you have to do in this life. You don't need us to tell you. We are here for you."

On hearing these words, I am disappointed. My guides are blocking me from entering the spirit realm. I had expected to meet with the Council of Elders, with the specific intent of finding out more about the reasons for my lifetime now. They were telling me that I already knew. I felt let down.

The session was supposed to have lasted over three hours, but only lasted an hour and a half.

Sitting in the regressionist's office afterwards, she was very excited about my experience, but I didn't share her euphoria. I felt annoyed at the wasted time and money. I left the building vowing never to go through the experience again.

However, I could not have envisaged what happened as soon as I opened the doors to exit the building. I was so overwhelmed by the experience that I contacted the regressionist at the first opportunity, once I'd arrived home.

It had started to rain. I didn't have an umbrella and so let the rain drops drip down my head and face until I was soaking wet. I didn't even notice them, as I walked the two kilometres back to the station. I was so absorbed in interpreting the messages being relayed to me by my guides, who flooded me with streams of castigatory statements that ran as strongly through me, as the raindrops did as they fell around me. The impact had been incredible. It had been like a blast of icy cold air smacking me in the face, followed by a tirade of aggressively delivered dialogue by both entities, yelling at me at the same time.

They never let up until I reached the station, and then they both suddenly left. Their messages that day were crystal clear. I knew what they meant. After Michael had passed, I had met with a clairvoyant to connect to him. Michael had told me that I know what I must do now in my life. He said, "I left, so that you could live your life."

Yes, I get it. I know the answers. I know my guides are with me, and I know that Michael is too. He returned to the spirit world so that he could help me now, from that realm.

I still had answers that I sought, though, despite the blocks my guides imposed on me that day. I still felt that a specialist regressionist should be able to facilitate me entering the spirit realm for the purposes and answers I sought.

A few months after this experience, I happened to read an account of someone else's Life Between Lives session. This person had sought the exact same answers about herself that I too felt were my questions. I felt that if she could discover these aspects of herself and the purposes for her current life journey, then I could too.

And so, it was that I made the trip to England to meet with this therapist.

This script is the unaltered script I wrote sitting on the plane from Heathrow to Sydney, whilst flying back from London.

Life Between Lives Script

At any one time on Earth only a handful of people are 'very special' souls. When I came to Australia in 1974, I came by myself, leaving all family behind. I had, had a difficult time during my life and sought a new life overseas. Australia offered me the opportunity to work in Sydney, which was a very exciting prospect. A few days after landing, and having acquired details of my teaching position, I headed out to meet with the Principal.

The first person I saw, as I entered the administration building of the school, was Michael (my husband to be). He had emigrated with his family five years before. Instantly I saw him, I knew that he was my soul mate. Our soul's connected.

Stepping back out of the administration building, I stepped into the next person who was to play a significant role in my life in Australia. This lady just happened to be casually walking to the staff room when our paths collided.

"I'm June Ralph," the lady smiled at me. "You must come to my house tonight for a party. Well, it's a staff get-together, actually," she beamed radiantly at me.

Of course, I went.

June became my Australian mum. She became 'nan' to my children, and I became her carer in her old age. She became my family from that day onwards.

June Ralph was one of the very special souls. She had that 'serene elegance of nature and selflessness' that surrounded her aura, emitting an ambience of spirit perfection. It was no coincidence that I met Michael and June that day – spirit had orchestrated it – I sensed this at the time.

June's life, however, was uneventful. She never married the man she truly loved – instead she married a man who couldn't give her children but allowed her freedom. I can see so clearly how my guides and planners selected June for the part she was to play in my life. I see now that June's main purpose in her life was to support me. If she had married the man she loved and had children, she would not have connected to me in the way that she did.

The Session

A 'Life Between Lives' regression is a complex procedure. The first part occurred the day prior to the regression, when I met with the hypnotherapist to chat about my expectations and for her to outline the process of how she operates. As I sat sipping tea in her lounge room, I felt a sense of ease and surety. It is an immensely exciting emotion to anticipate this journey of a most unusual nature.

The following day began early. As the session was to last for over five hours, it was important to allow ample time for the discussion elements as well as the actual time spent under hypnosis.

"Yes, I'm very comfortable. Thank you," I smile at the therapist as she wraps a blanket around me. She has lain me on a bed, positioned close to her recording chair. I close my eyes and let my mind go back into realms of my childhood, before she regresses me into the spirit realm. Again, I am surprised at not going deeper into a Beta or even a low Alpha state. Instead I feel as if I can wake up and be fully conscious at any time, during the session.

I feel quite relaxed, as I leave the Earth plane, soaring through eons of space and time, and sense that I am still 'me' but that I have no physical bodily form. This feeling is different from a past lives regression, where I watched scenes of events, rather like sitting in a movie theatre watching a movie, but which at every stage being aware of my own physical presence.

"I can see buildings floating around in space. Some of these structures knock into me and knock me off course."

"Yes, spirit frequently builds stuff and leaves it lying around," the therapist laughs.

"A bit like on Earth then!" I laugh with the lady as if we're back in her lounge room sipping tea on her sofa.

"What else can you see around you? Can you see any balls of energy?"

"Yes, I can see several groups of energy cells to each side of me, but they are not my cells."

"Hang on, when did I start calling these masses of soul groups, **cells**?"

"Susanna, talk to me about where you are headed, and let me know when you are there."

"Alright. I'm coming into a large colosseum building. It is very large and has long door openings all around, except there are no doors. I am entering one of these openings."

Immediately I enter the room, I see myself sitting at a desk, surrounded by massive tomes that I'm sorting through to locate information. I am very busy. Behind me Michael stands watching me as I place and replace books on shelves, handing him snippets of information every few seconds. Life in this place is extremely hectic – soul entities are coming and going like flashes of lightning. Each entering soul can only enter to the doorway – they are not permitted to enter the colosseum. I become aware that these souls are spirit guides. They come to collect the information from the researchers.

"So, I'm a researcher!" I suddenly yell out to the therapist. "I had presumed I was a teacher. I knew I wasn't a spirit guide!"

"What role does Michael play in this building?"

"He is the coordinator. Only he can cross the floor. He is the team leader. The researchers work in groups around the building and meet their spirit guides at the door to collect and give information."

"Do you know what you are researching?"

"Yes. Michael and I are currently intent on seeking strategies to help people with mental illness. We had reached a point, prior to us both incarnating, in which we could go no further in our research work in the spirit realm – we had to try them out for ourselves on Earth. The work we do is very indefinite. It is difficult to know how successful each strategy can be unless it is trialled."

Michael has since returned to continue our work.

"Did Michael ever seek to experience anything in his life with you that explored any of your strategies?"

"No, that was never Michael's role. As always, he is the Head Researcher – the coordinator and collector of information to pass on to the guides. In our life together, he was the one who always helped me see the bigger picture and put incidents into context."

"Can you see anyone else you know in this cell?"

"Yes, June has just come in to see me. She doesn't reside here. She is not part of my soul group. She just wants me to know she's there."

I smile at June and embrace her. She has a purple aura about her presence that shines in a kind of translucent light. Her aura emanates significant importance. Her visitation is brief – she's there to welcome me.

"Do the others in the room welcome you back?"

"No, it's as if I'm just there on a normal working day."

"Who else do you know?"

"As I turn around, away from June, I see my father sitting at a desk in the middle of the room. He is quietly sitting watching me and smiles as I face him. He is depicted as a very gentle soul, not strong in character or personality, which is what he was like on Earth."

"Susanna, I sense that something is now happening. Describe this to me."

"I am being led away by someone I don't know. He isn't my guide, but I sense that he is a male soul. We are now in a large auditorium where large screens are placed in various sections. Behind each screen are souls watching what is happening on their screens and chatting to their facilitators."

Facilitators? Where did that word come from?

"My facilitator," and that was exactly what he was, "has placed me in front of a blank screen. I look at the darkness and ask him what it means. He says that it's up to me what I want to choose in my next life. He also looks seriously at me, as he says that if I knew too much about my next life, I wouldn't incarnate."

I look back at him puzzled.

"I am now being taken to the Council of Elders."

"Susanna, how many are present?"

"Three. They are sitting in a line facing me, quite close. I can see their faces very clearly. They are wearing light beige robes and they are all male entities."

"Akra," one of the Elders speaks. "We gave you optimum opportunities in your life to do important things, but you chose to not achieve much. We gave you beauty, a doting husband, adoring children and a successful career, but you became lazy. Why was that?"

"I had an easy life. My husband adored me, but I didn't love him. We led an affluent life in which I didn't have to work, and so I chose to socialise instead."

"Akra, your next life needs to make better progress. Go back to the Viewing Room and write your script. Do not come back to us after your next life with the same story!"

"So, the Council is castigating you!" the therapist laughs out loud.

At this point in the proceedings I clearly hear her eating and drinking. I want to open my eyes and see what the delicious concoction is that she's drinking but know I must stay focused.

"Akra, Susanna, let's go to that lifetime," she says. "I'm intrigued as to why the Council is cross with you."

Almost immediately I see myself as a young girl of about twenty. The era is pre-World War 1. How do I know this? I just sense it, more from the dress of the time than from other visual signs.

I am wearing a long, flowing plain dress that is shaped right up to my neck. I have a kind of apron on top that covers most of my front body down to my knees. My hair is light brown in colour and pinned up in a high bun. I have a kind of silly looking hat on my head. I am walking into a very exclusive private school in England, as I have a meeting with the Headmaster. This is my first teaching position and I feel extremely nervous.

The next scene I am shown is a few years later, when I leave the school to have my first child. I am married now. My husband is a banker in London and earns a good salary. He tells me I don't have to work anymore.

My life is uneventful. I have everything I need, and we live in a beautiful house. I soon have three more children and we lead the typical life of the lower aristocracy. I am a beautiful woman, and as such attract attention to myself. This eventually leads to disagreements with my husband, but which are soon resolved when he passes suddenly from consumption.

I don't remarry, but instead take on work as a private tutor. This does not last long because my methods are different and cause conflict with others who require me to be more 'strict' and 'disciplined' in my teaching approaches. The last scene I am shown is a deathbed scene. My grandchildren are around the bed and kissing me goodbye.

"Deborah, I've seen this scene before – in a previous past life regression," I say to the therapist.

"This was shown to me as being a happy life, during the second of my regressions."

"So, Susanna, do you have any regrets about that lifetime?"

"Yes, I didn't achieve much. I was a teacher, but I was weak in how I saw my role. I had the ability to make effective change, but I took the easy path. I understand what the Council was eluding to. In my current life, I have to make up for that wasted life."

"What are you doing?" the lady sitting next to me on the flight from Singapore to Sydney asks me, as she peers over what I'm writing.

"I'm writing my script," I turn and look at her.

"I've never seen anyone write so fast!" she looked gobsmacked at me.

"That's because my spirit guides are downloading information to me that I have to write down quickly. They are very impatient with me, if I'm too slow!"

The lady looks even more perplexed and says, "I think you might be a very interesting lady to talk to. What do you do for a living?"

"I'm a teacher. What do you do?"

"I work with young people with mental health issues."

I smile as I recall the reason I am here on Earth in this lifetime. Of course, she does. Of course, that's why she's sitting next to me now.

We spend the next three hours chatting about mental health strategies.

Nothing is ever a coincidence!

Barriers

I have included this poem to conclude this set of sagas. Too often in our lives we build our own barriers by the way we choose to think or respond to people or situations. Sometimes these barriers are imposed on us, whether consciously, or inadvertently.

The one thing that I've discovered through delving deeply into my spiritual past is that we are very much in control of what we build. We make our own choices. We don't have to respond the way society expects us to. We don't have to build barriers – we can choose to bridge our connections, not just in this world, but through to the spirit world as well.

We interact with space in peculiar ways.
We run, dance and do somersaults when we play.
We can't see the barriers
That divide our world,
But that's not to say they're not there.

The barrier of time is of our own making.
We place stress and expectations on ourselves.
We don't think about reasons,
Except when we fail.
Don't we know pride leads to a fall?

The barrier of thought can affect our well-being.
A negative attitude can breed contempt.
We all want to be happy –
Too often we're not,
Because of the way that we think!

The barrier of love can be a bridge to life.
If we open our hearts in a caring way
By giving to those in need –
Our time and our love –
Then the light in our hearts will shine.

The barrier of race is a race against time.
We choose to treat other people differently.
Just because their skin's not white,
Or were born elsewhere
Does not give us this right of choice.

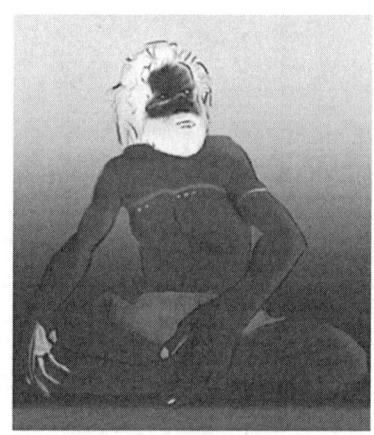

The barriers that deprive people of freedom
Take away rights and responsibilities.
We lose all our confidence –
And much self-esteem,
That portray lives without purpose.

So, recognise barriers by knocking down walls
And valuing diversity and difference.
We all want to be happy
And live useful lives
And know in our hearts that we cared.